I0834015

Gen. Grant is now the foremost figure in this war, and the whole nation is eager to know his history. The narrative of his rise from a very obscure and humble position to his present high command, illustrates the character of our institutions, and the certainty of the rewards assured to honest energy; and the eyes, not only of the whole country, but of the world, are now directed toward him. The biography before us gives a brief sketch of his early life, but is much more minute in detail of military operations since the war begun. The style is animated and graphic, and is well suited to its stirring theme.—*N. Y. Independent.*

In the "Hero Boy," Mr. Headley has made his work a labor of love and honor—love for the boys and honor for the man. Gathering his materials with great care, and arranging them with the skill of a practised hand, he has really produced the very best outline of the Lieutenant-General's career yet put in print; it is illustrated with maps, enriched with a glossary of military terms, and leads off admirably as the first of a series entitled "The Young American's Library of Modern Heroes."—*Chicago Journal.*

II.

THE PATRIOT BOY.

BEING THE

Life of Major-General O. M. Mitchel, the Astronomer and Hero.

1 vol., 16mo, cloth, 300 pages, fully illustrated. Price, $1.50

Extract from a letter received from Gen. Mitchel's Son.

Wm. H. Appleton, Esq.:

Dear Sir—I have read with great pleasure the life of my father, written by Rev. P. C. Headley, and just published by yourself. In every thing relating to the boyhood and early life of my father, the author has been most successful and correct.

Very respectfully, yours,

E. W. MITCHEL.

Notices of the Press.

General Mitchel was a remarkable man. As an astronomer, he was one of the foremost of the age; as an orator, he had few peers; while as a general, he proved himself possessed of the highest qualities of leadership. His nature was strong and magnetic; there was no resisting the fascination of his presence. He was idolized by his troops; and had he lived, he would doubtless have disputed the honors with the most successful of our chieftains.

We are glad the life of this gifted man has been written with reference to the youth of our country. We know it will do good, and stimulate many an ardent youth to noble endeavor. The present volume should be placed in the hands of every boy in the country; for the subject of it is one that cannot be too prominently kept before the eye of the nascent generation. It is got up in beautiful style, and reflects credit on the publisher.—*Albany Evening Journal.*

The career of one of the noblest characters America has yet produced. * * * "The Patriot Boy; or, the Life and Career of Major-General Ormsby M. Mitchel." It is written in the enthusiastic style of this author, who says in his preface that it is from authentic sources; and that in no important statement can the truthfulness of the narrative be questioned. The reader may here learn the leading incidents of Mitchel's romantic career. We know of none who presents a nobler example to the youth of America than the illustrious Mitchel.—*N. Y. Evening Post.*

We had once the pleasure of seeing the subject of this biography in his observatory in Cincinnati, where he most affably explained some of his methods of exploring the visible heavens. He was not then a soldier, but the patriotic love of country was active within him, ready to be called into action at his country's summons. He became a soldier—and an eminent one—and in the service he surrendered his life. As an astronomer, and as a general, he maintained a Christian life, and his death was a transit beyond the stars. Mr. Headley, who has succeeded so well in other biographies, has raised a fitting monument to the great and good man, and he directs the eyes of our youth to contemplate it.—*The Presbyterian.*

The subject is a brilliant example to American youth. We are familiar with the career of Prof. Mitchel, and rejoice to see it graphically portrayed in this beautiful volume. We would put this book into the hands of a lad to show him what true greatness there is in a man who has knowledge, religion, and patriotism. —*New York Commercial.*

III.

THE MINER BOY and his MONITOR.

Being the Life of Capt. John Ericsson, the Inventor,

DESIGNER OF THE FAMOUS IRON-CLAD "MONITOR," ETC.

A DEEPLY INTERESTING AND INSTRUCTIVE BOOK FOR BOYS.

One volume, 16mo, fancy cloth, 300 pages, fully illustrated. Price, $1.50.

Notices of the Press.

In his series of beautiful and useful Juveniles, Wm. H. Appleton, 92 Grand street, has last published "The Miner Boy and his Monitor," being the Life of John Ericsson, the inventor, by Headley, in which the story of that remarkable man is told with glowing enthusiasm, inspiring in the young reader a kindred appreciation. No recent career has been more crowded and, in one sense, oppressed with varied fortunes and extraordinary hazards and recoveries than that of Ericsson. It will amply repay study, and at the same time add to the stock of patriotic pride in a country which can welcome and encourage all who plant their foot on its soil.—*The New Yorker.*

The lives of Gens. Grant and Mitchel by the same author, were flatteringly received by the public, not by boys alone, but of grown up people as well. The idea of placing our prominent and most deserving men in a historic light before the actions which have made them illustrious are deprived of their freshness, is certainly a happy one; and the practised pen of Mr. Headley is just the one to produce biographies worthy of the subjects sketched. There is as much romance for the general reader, old or young, in the life of John Ericsson as in that of George Stephenson, and we undertake to say that the author has in the present instance been as faithful to the ingenious Swede as to the talented biographer of the great railway man was to him. The text of this pretty volume is liberally illustrated, which never fails to heighten the interest of reading boys.—*Troy Daily Whig.*

We have no hesitation in saying that this is the most interesting and romantic of all the recent "boy books." It treats of a personage whose name is far more familiar to our people than his history—of a man who belongs to that class of great mechanics who are equally important and useful in war or in peace. Of course, it will be said that the life of Ericsson is an example to boys, and it is, as far as industry, honesty, and energy go; but it is of special interest to boys who have a genius for mechanics, and, in any event, is most entertaining and instructive reading.—*N. Y. Evening Post.*

A fascinating history of a man of remarkable inventive genius to whom the nation is under immeasurable obligation. None can tell what course the war might have taken, or what result might have been reached, had not the monster Merrimac been checked by the Monitor, and her early success turned into defeat in the ever-memorable battle at Hampton Roads. The great influence of Ericsson's genius in manifold inventions is also shown, and many interesting things are told concerning Sweden, his native land.—*Congregationalist.*

LIFE AND NAVAL CAREER

OF

VICE-ADMIRAL

DAVID GLASCOE FARRAGUT.

Midshipman Farragut entering the service on board the Essex. Frontispiece. See p. 21.

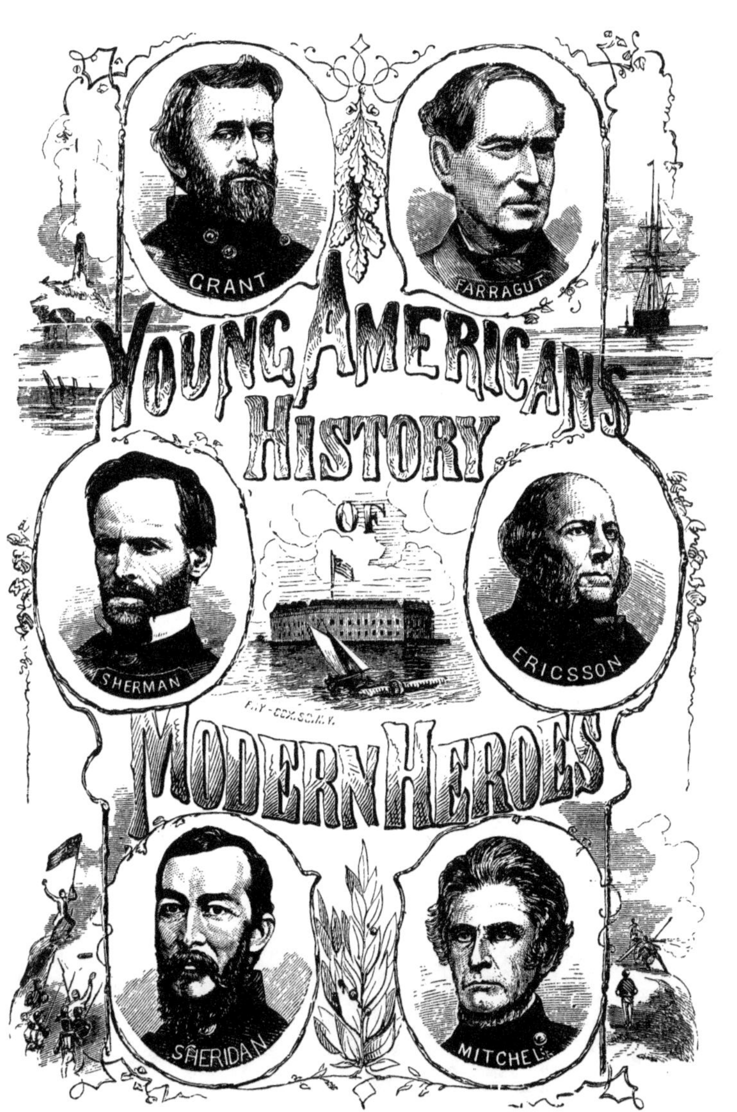
GRANT
FARRAGUT
YOUNG AMERICANS
HISTORY
OF
SHERMAN
ERICSSON
MODERN HEROES
SHERIDAN
MITCHEL

LIFE AND NAVAL CAREER

OF

VICE-ADMIRAL

DAVID GLASCOE FARRAGUT.

BY

REV. P. C. HEADLEY,

AUTHOR OF "NAPOLEON," "JOSEPHINE," "WOMEN OF THE BIBLE," "HERO BOY," "PATRIOT BOY," "LIFE OF SHERMAN," ETC., ETC.

NEW YORK:
WILLIAM H. APPLETON, 92 & 94 GRAND STREET.
1865.

TO THE

MIDSHIPMEN OF THE AMERICAN NAVY,

THIS

RECORD OF AN ILLUSTRIOUS CAREER,

WHOSE BEGINNING WAS A FAITHFUL PERFORMANCE OF THE

DUTIES WHICH BELONG TO THEIR RANK,

IS INSCRIBED

BY

THE AUTHOR.

PREFACE.

The sketch of the great naval commander of the age is added to the biographies of military heroes for youth, because his life is an unquestioned example of an honorable and most successful career. To some of the sources of information the author was referred by the Admiral himself.

The material for the sketch of the Admiral's early history are not so full as might be desired. His life on the sea necessarily made it quite impossible to gather many incidents of interest in connection with his subsequent career, which would have become traditionary in a community where the years of boyhood and youth were passed.

The "Journal" of Commodore David Porter, of the Essex, Abbott's "History of the Rebellion," and the "Army and Navy Journal," have been valuable works of reference.

Life on board a man-of-war, and facts in regard to the last conflict with England, are given, to interest the youthful reader, and shed light on the career of the boy-midshipman in the earlier period of the American navy. To our Vice-Admiral the sudden and rapid growth of our marine power during the four years past, must be a marvellous contrast with the small progress made during the half century of his previous service in it.

This record of his long experience, and the gigantic greatness of our present naval force, is offered to the youthful reader with the hope that he will find both instruction and entertainment, and that it will aid him in the formation of a patriotic and Christian character, whatever the profession or calling chosen for the activity of manhood.

CONTENTS.

CHAPTER XI.

CHAPTER XII.

CHAPTER XIII.

CHAPTER XIV.

CHAPTER XV.

CHAPTER XVI.

CHAPTER XVII.

CHAPTER XVIII.

CHAPTER XIX.

CHAPTER I.

The Island-Home of the Farragut Family—Mahon and Ciudadella—Removal to the New World—The Name in the Revolutionary War—David's Birth—Early Love of the Sea—His Fearless Spirit.

THE Farragut family were originally from Catalonia. This province lies on the Spanish coast, and along the Pyrènees; its "blushing vineyards, verdant landscapes, and its whitewashed villages," glowing in the sunlight, before the traveller's delighted eye, while the ship that bears him onward toward Marseilles, or some less noted port on the sea-border of France, cuts the waves of the blue Mediterranean.

Southeasterly, and nearly midway between Spain and Africa, and opposite the kingdom of Valencia, are the Balearic Islands, now a province of Spain. The largest is Majorica, the second Minorica, the third Ivica, with two smaller ones, Formentera and Cobrera. Minorica was the island-home of George Farragut, our Admiral's father.

These sea-girdled lands were first settled by the ancient Phœnicians, and successively fell into the hands of the Rhodians and Carthagenians. The leader of the last-mentioned, Hanno, founded Mago, called Mahon, and Tamnon or Ciudadella, on the opposite extremities of Minorica.

The Romans added the Balearic Islands to their Empire 123 B. C., and held them for five and a half centuries. Then they were seized by the Vandals, who swept over Europe, and still later by the Goths. At length the Moors became the possessors of them, and they have been for a long period quietly under the sceptre of Spain.

Ciudadella was the capital of Minorica, and the residence of Mr. Farragut. It is about thirty miles from Mahon, and is still the favorite town of the nobility and gentry. You will be interested in a lively description of the people and scenery of the island from the pen of a young official on board a man-of-war, an instructor of midshipmen, of whom you will learn more hereafter. He sailed in the U. S. Frigate Constellation.

"To an American, whose land smiles with plenty, one of the most striking contrasts Minorica presents, is its extreme poverty. Proofs of this meet you on all hands, and in every shape. You see them in the number of mendicants that crowd the streets, in the modes to which many of the inhabitants resort to obtain subsistence, in the fare to which they are obliged to submit, and in the low prices affixed to manual labor and domestic services. As you pass through the town, hosts of ragged boys whose pertinacity no refusal can overcome, follow you from street to street, with faces wrinkled into a thousand shapes of woe, and with the incessant whining cry of 'Officer, give me one penny for de bread—I say, Officer, give me one penny.'

"There is another class of beggars, composed of old men and women, who, from age or infirmity, are unable to work, and therefore really necessitous. Such have stated times for asking alms, which are on Saturdays and some of the Church holidays. They go from house to house, generally visiting only the families to whom they are known. They never enter, but tell their tale of poverty and suffering without; at the same time beseeching some trifling gratuity for the 'love of God and the blessed Virgin.' To the honor of that portion of the inhabitants who are in better circumstances, it must be mentioned that they are rarely turned away without an alms.

"I used frequently to walk out in the country, and, go in whatever direction I might, it rarely happened that I did not see a number of persons carefully gathering up the ordure in the roads for the purpose of selling it. Multitudes of the inhabitants have no regular means of subsistence, but lounge about in the public places, ready to engage in any temporary or menial service that may offer itself to them. In some parts of the island there are many whose only bread is barley cakes, and the number is not small of those who cannot obtain even these, but are compelled to subsist almost exclusively on fish, fruits, and vegetables.

"In one of my rambles into the country I lost my way, and came to a place where an old man was repairing a stone wall. I begged him to direct me. He replied that he was going to dinner, and could accompany me on my way toward Mahon. Arrived opposite a little stone hut, he said, 'There is my home; I am going to dine; will you dine with me?' I declined. The old gentleman insisted, and I at length yielded. The table was an old bench resembling the movable seats in some of the schoolhouses in New England; and the chairs were other benches of the same kind, only a little lower. The dinner consisted of a small loaf of brown bread, a bowl of vegetable soup, a bit of old sausage, and a little cheese, with the common red wine of the country. An old rusty knife and fork, neither of which had a handle, two or three broken plates, a tumbler, and a gourd-shell, constituted the whole furniture of the table. As the reader may guess, I ate but little, but I thought the more; and I could not but be deeply affected, as Fancy pictured to my view the multitudes in that rocky and sterile island who were accustomed to sit down to a worse dinner than even that before me; whilst in my own loved and happy land the family could scarcely be found who were obliged to submit to such fare. The old gentleman's family consisted only of himself and his wife. I was touched with their unaffected kindness and the patriarchal simplicity of their manners. They did not seem to dream that the dinner to which they had invited me was not a dinner for a king, and they expressed a thousand regrets that I had not a better appetite. It is but justice to add that my kind-hearted host positively refused the slightest remuneration for his hospitality.

"Minorica produces in abundance grapes, oranges, figs, pomegranates, olives, apricots, melons, cauliflowers, and various other fruits and vegetables, and the money received in exchange for them is nearly all that gets into the island."

Did you ever hear of wood being sold by *weight?* It is done there, and at a very high price. Charcoal is more generally burnt, and the fire is made in a *copa*, the Spanish name of a pan for holding coals in the middle of the room, over which the children shiver on the cooler days of the year, when the streets will be lined with these copas, put out in the air to ignite the charred wood before removing them to the frosty rooms.

The early inhabitants, with those of the other Balearic Islands, were remarkable for their skill in using, like David the son of Jesse, the *sling;* and among the countrymen great expertness, it is said, is still common. To make their sons good marksmen it was a custom of parents to hang the breakfast upon boughs of lofty trees, to remain there till brought down by the boys with the sling. The strong arms of manhood, thus trained, would hurl with tremendous power the "smooth stones." When the warriors went into battle, a sling was suspended from the neck, another from the waist, and a third carried in the hand for immediate use.

Both men and women are excellent swimmers. One of the latter, when a man-of-war had lain becalmed off the coast, became impatient for the penny a basket of fruit would procure, and, plunging in with the luxury, swam safely to the ship.

You will see female porters in the streets of the towns, with a heavy burden on their heads and a *distaff* in their hands, and shoes with wooden soles on their feet, making a strange clatter, and sometimes startling you with the impression that a donkey is behind you. A cow and jackass, and a horse and mule, are harnessed together. Wheel carriages have never been used in Minorica, the backs of animals being the substitutes; and when you mount to ride into the country the boys will chase you for miles to get a copper for holding the horse, mule, or donkey when you stop.

There are many other curious customs and scenes in Minorica. In a cathedral at Mahon is a magnificent organ, in strength and sweetness of tone surpassed by few instruments in the world. Of course the people of these isles are Catholics, and have all the display, monkish beggary, and superstition of papal countries where but little progress has been made in education.

Such was the isolated land which became too limited for the mind and heart of George Farragut, whose aspirations for greater freedom led him to our shores.

It was in the memorable year 1776 that he came to this country, and entered the American army. That he was a good soldier the inherited qualities of his son, and the rank of major to which he attained, assure us.

When victory over our British foe—whose aristocratic pride has not lost its hostility to freedom here—gave to the colonies victory and nationality, George Farragut retired from military service, and decided to establish

"A local habitation and a name,"

under the banner he had defended in battle. He married Miss Elizabeth Shine, of North Carolina. She had also a distinguished origin, belonging to the Scotch family of McIven. Like the parents of nearly all the great commanders in the civil war, he became a Western pioneer. He selected lands near Knoxville, Tennessee, whose particular locality is known as Campbell's Station. Here he lived a worthy representative of the "hunters of Kentucky," who have in Colonel Daniel Boone a leader of world-wide fame.

You have read the stories of frontier life. Major Farragut had to keep the loaded gun at hand day and night, making his clearing a fortress and farm. The stealthy savage was lurking around, and he could not tell when the hostile hand might send the arrow or bullet to his very door.

Here, the day succeeding the twenty-fifth anniversary of the Declaration of Independence, July 5th, 1801, a son was born, who was named David Glascoe Farragut.

Major Farragut left the quiet of the land for the sea; and it is not strange that David caught the romance of its adventure, and with boyish impatience longed to be on the ocean wave. He dreamed of ships and battles, and was impatient for the hour when he might wear the jacket of the sailor boy. All his earliest recollections were of the wild border experience, which gave to his naturally daring spirit that fearlessness characteristic of him in the heroic deeds of riper years. It was not blind rashness, which in young and old is sometimes mistaken for intelligent courage; but an ingrained indifference to peril, when a worthy object demanded a given course of action. Not only so, but he was obedient and uncorrupted by vicious habits—winning the confidence of friends, and laying the foundation of greatness unsullied with selfish and sensual indulgence.

CHAPTER II.

David is appointed Midshipman—Life on board a Man-of-war—The Decks—Mess-room—Divisions of Time—The Officers—Midshipmen—Their Promotion.

THE pioneer's son loved the wild slopes of the Cumberland Mountains and the hunter's trail. He found a strange delight in the romantic and varied scenes familiar to the settlers on the new lands of our vast domain; but his spirit's longing for the scarcely more perilous and open plains of the mariner's toil and honors, must be gratified. The fond father hesitated—delayed; but at last yielded, and a midshipman's warrant was obtained and placed in his boyish hand.

You can imagine his delight, for you have known the rapture of success in some favorite and difficult plan of early ambition. Nor was his joy diminished by the fact that he was to sail with his father's familiar friend, Captain Porter, of the Essex.

Before I tell you of him and his good ship, you may

want to know more about the duties and trials of a mid-shipman, in the then *young* navy of the United States, and the officers of a man-of-war. Let us look into a man-of-war, so long the home of David, and see the arrangements, and know the officers that rule over the floating military kingdom.

A frigate has three decks. The first is called the spar deck, which is again divided into three distinct departments: the quarter-deck, the forecastle, and the booms. The quarter-deck is next to the cabin in importance. To appear there the officer on duty must be dressed in full uniform, and touch his hat as a sign of respect when he ascends to it from below, or comes over the ship's sides. Writes the schoolmaster of the "middies" on board of the Constitution: "I have been reprimanded for walking there in a hot summer's day without a cravat on, and the etiquette of touching the hat is in some instances so rigorously exacted that midshipmen are suspended or quarantined for neglecting to comply with it. No officer is allowed to be seated on the quarter-deck, and loud laughter and boisterous conversation are strictly prohibited. I knew an officer high in rank to be reported to the commodore by a master commandant for breaking out into what he called a 'horse laugh' on the quarter-deck. In port the starboard side of the quarter-deck is appropriated to the captain and wardroom officers, and the larboard to the inferior officers. As you stand facing the ship's head the starboard is on your right and larboard on your left. The larboard is also called *port*.

"I have seen a sailor taken to the gangway and receive 'a dozen' for walking aft on the starboard side of the deck. At sea the higher officers are entitled to the weather side, that is, the side upon which the wind blows, whichever it may be."

You will notice three stairway openings, called hatches, on the quarter-deck, of which the after one, or that nearest the vessel's stern, belongs entirely to the superior officers. The capstan, or wooden cylinder near the centre, is turned to lift the anchor and other heavy weights. Before the mizzenmast is the wheel, in charge of four men, by which the helm is controlled and the ship kept in her course over the waves. In front of it are the binacles, or boxes, containing each a mariner's compass.

Do you ask, "Why are there two?" To be more secure; for if one should fail by any defect or accident, another is left to guide the commander. The favorite haunt of the men is the forecastle, or the part of the spar-deck forward of the foremast, or nearest the prow. Here they assemble at evening in summer time, and "spin their yarns," sing songs, and dance, forgetful of the unpleasant scenes and toils of their monotonous round of duty. Then, again, recollections of home and friends afar, will soften down the tone of social enjoyment, and bring the tear to the eye which had often looked fearlessly upon the wildest storm-cloud and the wrathful billow.

A blacksmith's shop is carried on the frigate, which is moved to the forecastle when there is work for its fire and hammer. Between this and the quarter-deck are stored extra spars, and all the boats excepting five—one at the stern, and one at each of the quarters. This lumber-room is called the "booms."

Passing by some other fixtures which you will understand better by seeing them, and asking a kind sailor to tell you their uses and names, we will go to the main, or gun-deck, the "great luxury of a frigate." It is covered, and neither sun, rain, nor dew can prevent or annoy the fine promenade it affords. On a warm day or moonlight evening, nothing can be more delightful to the mariner than to walk the floor of the floating hall, and feel the cooling breeze, and look out on the changeful sea. But we have not seen the most important place in the ship—the seat of power, the throne of the sea-king—the captain's *cabin*. It occupies almost the whole room in the main deck, abaft or back of the mizzenmast, and covers the space of four guns, separated from the rest of the deck by "bulkheads," as partitions on shipboard are called. These wooden walls are removed when the vessel is cleared, or got ready for action, for the deck then becomes a battle-field.

The half-deck extends from the cabin to the mainmast, and on the larboard side, is common to all the officers, and in warm weather is the general reading-room. The "waist" is the part before the mainmast, appropriated to the carpenters, tailors, shoemakers, &c. Next comes the galley, right back of the foremast, which is the ship's *kitchen.* In one part is the cooking, which is divided into three departments, one of which is for the captain, and the others for the subordinate officers. The back part of the galley is called the "coppers," and belongs to the crew. Upon the sides of the galley are tables for the cooks, each having his place, and defended against any invasion by his neighbor, often with all the earnestness, rising sometimes to violence, of the most indignant defender of insulted honor.

By quite a natural transition from the kitchen, we go forward of the foremast, and find the farm-yard of the frigate—the sheep, goats, pigs and poultry—a sight which might remind us of Barnum's "Happy Family." You will also see pumps for raising the bilge water, salt water to wash the ship, and to procure the fresh water from below.

And now we will go down another ladder. Here we are on the *berth* deck. Our feet are below water mark, and he who is not fond of hard knocks must look out for his head. The after part of the berth deck is occupied as a mess-room by the lieutenants and other commissioned officers. It is called the wardroom, extends to a considerable distance forward of the mizzenmast, and is separated from the rest of the deck by a bulkhead. It has five state-rooms on each side, which, though not very large, are sufficiently commodious, and are furnished with neat little bureaus at the public expense. Some of the officers have them carpeted and fitted up in elegant style. The first lieutenant is entitled to the first state-room on the starboard side, and the others follow him in the order of their rank. The room on the larboard side, corresponding with the first lieutenant's, belongs to the sailing master, and the purser, surgeon, and chaplain are entitled to rooms receding from his in the order in which their names are here mentioned.

The wardroom receives its light principally from a large skylight overhead. Immediately forward of the wardroom is the steerage, the midshipmen's domicile. This differs materially in different ships. In some, as in the Constellation, it is partitioned off into different mess-rooms; while in others, as in the Brandywine, it is all common, and is separated from the forward part of the deck only by a canvas curtain. In the Constellation, as already mentioned, there are four mess-rooms, two on each side of the ship. They are each about nine feet by seven. The "*middies*" are not allowed to have trunks on board, and the mess-rooms are therefore furnished with lockers to supply their place. Of these there are two kinds, chest lockers and "up and down" lockers. The chest lockers are nothing more than boxes surrounding three sides of the rooms; the upright ones are more like bureaus, and are much more commodious.

Time on shipboard is divided into watches, and reckoned by bells. Hence you never hear the question, "What o'clock?" but "How many bells is it?" The twenty-four hours are divided into six equal portions, called watches. At the end of the first half-hour of one of these portions, the bell is struck one; at the end of the second, two; and so on till the series reaches eight, when it commences again. Thus it will be perceived that two bells means either one, five, or nine o'clock; and five bells either half-past two, six, or ten. In the ship's journals the dates are put down according to the common mode of reckoning time. The division of time into watches differs somewhat at sea and in port. In the former case, the watches are all four hours long, with the exception of two in the evening, called dog-watches, from four to six, and from six to eight. In port there is but one watch during the day, viz., from eight o'clock A. M. to eight P. M. The night watches are the same as at sea.

Order is the first great rule on board a man-of-war, and that to which all others must bend. It is, in fact, the Alpha and the Omega, the beginning and the ending, the centre and the circumference of her whole internal organization. "To every thing there is a season, and a time to every purpose under heaven." From day to day, from week to week, from month to month, and from year to year, the same stroke of the bell is followed by the same whistle, the same call, and the recurrence of the same duties. Every thing has its place, too, and must be kept in it. So true is this, that a person acquainted with the details of a ship can lay his hand on a given object in any part of her, as well in the dark as if a thousand suns were shining on it.

"The three grand divisions of the moral elements in the naval service are into officers, men, and marines. Of the former there are generally about forty, of the second somewhat more than three hundred, and of the latter thirty-five, more or less.

"An anecdote, related by a gentleman in Mahon, is so much to the purpose here, that I cannot forbear to repeat it. It so happened that one of the men concerned in the murder of a French lieutenant was a southern negro, and a perfect Ninevite in knowledge. In the course of the trial it became necessary for him to take an oath, and an oath and the Copernican system were all one to him. So the court set about enlightening him. 'Don't you acknowledge a Supreme Being?' 'Supreme Being! massa,' replied Cuff, 'I no stand what he mean.' 'God, your Creator, the Being who made us all; don't you acknowledge any superior Being?' 'O, yes, massa, my *Captain*.'"

You smile at the poor African whose thoughts of God

rose no higher than the monarch of a frigate—kept in pagan darkness; but you will not forget a common Father made you to differ in His Providence, and has declared that "Ethiopia shall stretch forth her hands unto God."

CHAPTER III.

More about the Men of a Man-of-war—First Lieutenant—The Purser—The Surgeon—The Midshipmen—The Quartermaster--Boatswain—Gunners—Mechanics—The Government of the Frigate.

NEXT to the Captain, is the First Lieutenant in rank, whose duties are quite equal in responsibility to those of his superior. He must inspect every part of the ship, exercise the men at the guns, see that they are neatly and properly clad, and that the little world afloat is in perfect order. Whenever the sails are to be reefed in the gale, or the anchor moved, he holds the trumpet and issues the command. No officer requires more versatile talent and elevated character to fill well his position.

The Purser keeps the keys of the treasury, and all the provisions on board are in his charge. Surely he ought to be an *honest* man, or he will speculate out of the extensive business in his hands.

The Surgeon and two assistants are the medical staff

of a frigate. The latter have a position of their own, ranking next above the midshipmen. The Surgeon must report every morning the number, diseases, and names of the sick.

We come now to the rank of DAVID GLASCOE FARRAGUT, when his name was enrolled in the list of officers connected with the Essex—the midshipman. "Young gentlemen," is a naval term applied to the midshipmen, or, as contracted, "the middies." The number of these varies from twelve to upwards of twenty. It would be difficult to give any very definite idea of what their duties are: for, although an interesting class of officers on account of what they *are to be*, yet in their present capacity they do little more than echo the orders of their superiors. There is a change of wind; the officer of the deck issues the command to "lay aft to the braces." "Lay aft to the braces!" cries every midshipman on deck. The wind freshens, so as to make it necessary to clew up the mainsail; "Man the main cluegarnet!" is thundered through the trumpet. "Man the main clue-garnet!" is instantly repeated by some half dozen echoes. However, they have some specific duties. They carry messages from the officer of the deck to the captain, and in port one of them takes charge of every boat that leaves the ship. At sea, seven bells is reported to them every morning at half-past eleven o'clock, when they are obliged to go on deck with their quadrants and take the sun. They have to work out the last day's run, and report the course, distance made good, and ship's place at noon each day to the captain. They muster the crew when the watch is called at night. They are also required to keep a journal of the cruise, which is, however, only a copy of the ship's log. This is examined every few weeks by the commanding officer, and if it happens not to be written up when called for, the delinquent is generally punished by a curtailment of some of his indulgences.

The number of midshipmen and passed midshipmen in the navy of the United States is limited to four hundred and sixty-four. The appointments to the naval schools preparatory to this position, are distributed among the States and Territories. Each candidate must be over fourteen, and under eighteen years of age, and a resident of the Congressional District from which he is sent. Indeed, the regulations in regard to their examination and admission to the course of study, are similar to those which govern the selection of cadets and their entrance into the military academy. The travelling expenses of the accepted young man are paid by the Government from his residence to the school, and five hundred dollars allowed annually for current expenses. The course of instruction covers four years, and includes mathematics, astronomy, navigation, surveying, ethics, French, Spanish, drawing, artillery and infantry tactics, seamanship, naval gunnery, the steam engine, and other branches of science.

Besides, during the term of years, two cruises of about three months each are made in a ship-of-war for instruction, when the boys have a kind of pleasure excursion, visiting various ports and getting a taste of salt-water life. When they graduate, they receive "warrants as midshipmen," and their rank is according to their order of merit. If, after two years of service from this time, they pass examination before a board of three captains and two commanders, for promotion, showing proficiency in practical navigation, the management of the steam-engine and gunnery, they have warrants as *passed midshipmen* awarded them, with a larger salary.

And now the way is fairly open to the "middies" for the higher position of master, lieutenant, commander, captain, commodore, and admiral.

When young Farragut entered the navy there was a shorter way; for naval schools in this country were unknown. The institution at Annapolis, Maryland, was removed, when the rebellion darkened around it, to Newport, Rhode Island, but will probably be soon transferred again to the former and original place.

"The office of quartermaster is one of some dignity and considerable importance. Its duties are not laborious, but they require vigilance, carefulness, judgment, and a thorough acquaintance with practical seamanship.

In port only one of them keeps watch on deck at a time. You may know him by his spy-glass, and his busy, bustling air. He is all eye and all locomotion. He cocks his telescope at every new object that appears, and gives it a thorough scrutiny. It is his duty to keep a look-out for signals from other ships, and to report them to the officer of the deck; and also to report to him all boats that come alongside, and all other movements and occurrences in the harbor which he may deem of sufficient importance. At sea, two of the quartermasters are required to be on deck during the day, and half of them at night. One is stationed at the wheel to steer the ship, and the others keep a look-out as in port. When the log is thrown, they hold the minute glass. They have to strike the bell every half hour, and take turns in mixing and serving the grog. In entering and leaving a harbor, when it is necessary to sound, one of them is stationed in each of the main-chains to heave the lead. All the colors and signals are under their charge.

"The boatswain, gunner, carpenter, and sailmaker, form a distinct class of officers, called forward officers. The boatswain is charged with the rigging of the ship, and in port attends to squaring the yards. You may know him by his silver whistle, rattan cane, and above all, by the ruddy hues of his countenance, and the odious vapors that issue from his mouth. The gunner has charge of the military stores, and, when all hands are called off, of the main rigging. The carpenter is responsible for the stores belonging to his department, and superintends the corking of the ship and other work performed by his subalterns. The sailmaker is charged with the sails, hammocks, and generally all the canvas in the ship. At sea he is obliged to go aloft on each of the three masts, examine the condition of the sails, and report it to the first lieutenant every morning before breakfast.

"Each of the boatswain's mates has a silver whistle suspended from his neck, with which he echoes the orders of his superiors. He has a different pipe for almost every important order that can be given. For instance, there is one for calling all hands, another for hoisting away, a third for hauling taught and belaying, and so on of others. Amid the darkness and fury of the tempest, when the orders of the trumpet are drowned by the loud uproar of the elements, the shrill pipe of the boatswain's whistle reaches the ear of the sailor on the top of the highest mast, and no language could convey to him a more definite meaning than its well-known tones. The duty of the quarter-gunners is to keep the guns and all other things belonging to the gunner's department in proper order. They have to inspect the guns frequently to see that every thing about them is well secured, and at night report their condition to the officer of the deck every two hours. When all hands are called to reef or furl sails, the quarter-gunners and quartermasters are charged with the mainyard. The armorer is the ship's blacksmith. The cooper opens the provision barrels when their contents are wanted, and performs other matters in his line of business, when necessary. The duties of a cook are somewhat arduous, and it requires a good deal of patience and care to perform them acceptably to the crew. The meals must always be reported "ready" at seven bells, morning, noon, and night. At noon, when dinner is reported ready, the cook takes a specimen to the officer of the deck, who inspects it to see that it is properly cooked. The cockswain is designed for the captain's boat, but our commanders sometimes select a quartermaster or other trustworthy person to perform the duties of cockswain. There are two other subordinates who have not even the rank of petty officers. They are the ship's corporals. They take turns in keeping watch at night on the gun-deck, and their duty is to see that no light is burning in any part of the ship where it is not allowed. They make an hourly report to the officer of the deck.

"In regard to the rest of the crew, the seamen generally compose about one-half. Those of this rank must have seen a good deal of sea service, and are supposed to be thoroughly acquainted with practical navigation. If they are found to be greatly deficient in this respect, they are degraded. They receive twelve dollars per month, and are appointed to the most honorable and responsible stations in the ship. They have a good deal of the pride of profession, entertaining the utmost contempt for all who do not know what salt water and heavy gales are. The ordinary seamen receive ten dollars per month. They must have had some experience in naval matters, but are neither expected nor required to be finished sailors. Promotions from the rank of ordinary seamen to that of seamen are not frequent.

"There was no part of the system on board a man-of-war that interested me more than the distribution of power, and the complete subordination of rank. Persons have no idea of the perfection of military government. Every officer in the navy can say to every one below him, "Go," and he goeth, and "Do this," and he doeth. There is no quibbling or higgling about the matter at all, his will and pleasure are in the place of all argument. Not only is the captain of a public vessel supreme, but every other officer is in some sense a despot; for where he gives an order to an inferior officer or man, it must be obeyed, though it contradict a previous order received from a superior. The officer who gives the last order is in that case responsible for the disobedience of the first. I recollect a fact which will serve to illustrate this principle. The first lieutenant of one of our ships had given orders to a tailor not to do any work for the midshipmen without his permission, at the same time sending word to the midshipman to that effect. One of them, who happened to be absent from the ship at the time, a few days after wished to have some garment repaired, and ordered the tailor to do it. He refused. The midshipman insisted, and the worthy knight of the goose stoutly persisted in his refusal. The spirited young officer reported him to the first lieutenant, who had him flogged for disobedience."

There is another thing on shipboard which will interest you—the *signals*. If one vessel wishes to hold conversation with another at a distance, a flag is raised with certain figures upon it, which refer to words in the signal-book. If a commander desires to invite the officer of a ship in sight of his own to dine with him at a given hour, he has only to put out the flag with the right figures, and the invited captain turns to his book and finds the words, till he spells out the friendly message, and then answers in the same way. Such, in a general view, is the round of activity on board of a frigate, and you can see just where young Farragut had his post of duty when a mere boy. But he started right, showing no disposition to chafe against the stern restraints of naval command. Cheerful subjection to authority was the first and most important lesson, the grand step in the life-march of a noble ambition.

CHAPTER IV.

Midshipman Farragut at Sea—The American Navy at that time—The War with England—The Essex—Her first Cruise.

THE delay attending Midshipman Farragut's appointment brought his entrance upon life in the navy within a few months of the second war with England. The year 1811 was a period of comparative quiet in our small naval force, and, excepting the novelty of his new experience, and the practical lessons he was learning, had nothing to make it memorable.

The United States navy was reduced to *twenty* vessels and a few gunboats. Two of these were not seaworthy; and another, the Oneida, was on Lake Ontario; leaving only *seventeen* ships of war, in 1812, to defend the national rights upon the ocean. The names of the vessels were:

Constitution,	44 guns.	Congress,	38 guns.
President,	44 "	Constellation,	38 "
United States.	44 "	Chesapeake,	38 "

New York,	36 guns.	Argus,	16 guns.
Essex,	32 "	Siren,	16 "
Adams,	28 "	Oneida,	16 "
Boston,	28 "	Vixen,	14 "
John Adams,	28 "	Enterprise,	14 "
Wasp,	18 "	Nautilus,	14 "
Hornet,	18 "	Viper,	12 "

The gunboats which "first appeared afloat in 1805" on our waters carried one and two guns. In April, 1806, fifty of them were ordered by a law of Congress.

This means of warfare we employed in the cannonading of Tripoli in 1804, obtaining them from Naples; but on account of their imperfection, we built some of our own. They would look like toys beside the iron-clads of modern invention, and very soon disappear before the heavy shot of these mailed leviathans of the deep.

Do you ask "Why was our navy so weak?" It was strange indeed that the Government, after the experience of three conflicts, reddening the sea with the blood of our heroic tars, should neglect this arm of the service, till we had the mere fragment of a navy never large, with which to meet the uneasy, threatening monarchies of Europe. We had fought victoriously, between 1776 and 1806, England, France, and the Barbary States. Then the exhaustion of strength and political strife almost paralyzed Government, just when the greatest preparations for aggressions and united vigilance, were needed. We had of ficers equal in ability and successful valor to any in the world; but they were worthless without ships of war.

Just at this crisis, when Farragut consecrated his young life to the country on the sea, the signs of another conflict with England gave a new impulse to the declining strength of the navy. And that you may understand more fully the exciting period in American history which stirred the loyal spirit of the sailor boy, and also the feeling and course of England which has been again apparent in the rebellion now closed, I will add a statement of the causes of the renewed appeal to arms so soon after the Revolutionary War.

Great Britain had lavished men and money in the terrible struggle with France, and become weakened by the losses sustained. "Her war-ships stretched from Copenhagen to the Nile, and to supply these with seamen she resorted to impressment, not only on her own shores, amid her own subjects, but on American ships, among American sailors. Our merchant vessels were arrested on the high seas, and men, on the groundless charge of being deserters, immediately coerced into the British service. To such an extent was this carried that in *nine months* of the years 1796 and '97 Mr. King, the American Minister at London, had made application for the release of *two hundred and seventy-one seamen*, most of whom were American citizens.

"At first the British Government claimed only the right

to seize deserters; but its necessities demanding a broader application to right of search, her vessels of war arrested American merchantmen to seek for *British seamen*, and later still for British subjects; finally every sailor was obliged to prove himself a citizen of the United States on the spot, or he was liable to be forced into British service. American merchants were thus injured while prosecuting a lawful commerce, and, worse than all, great distress was visited on the friends and relatives of those who were illegally torn from their country and pressed into the hated service of a hated nation. Over six thousand were known to have been thus seized, while the actual number was much greater.

"Not content with committing these outrages on the high seas, English vessels boarded our merchantmen and impressed our seamen in our own waters. That line which runs parallel to the seacoast of every nation, and which is considered its legitimate boundary, presented no obstacles to British cruisers.

"In 1804 the frigate Cambria boarded an American merchantman in the harbor of New York, and in direct opposition to the port officers carried off several of her seamen. To complete the insult, the commander declared, in an official letter to the British minister, that he 'considered his ship, while lying in the harbor of New York, as *having dominion around her within the distance of her buoys*.' Not long after a coasting vessel, while going from one American port to another, was hailed by a British cruiser, and, refusing to stop, was fired into and one of her crew killed. Thus an American citizen was murdered within a mile of shore, and while going from port to port of his own country.

"These aggressions on land and insults at sea continued, at intervals, down to 1806, when our commerce received a more deadly blow from the British orders in council, and Napoleon's famous Berlin and Milan decrees. To annoy and cripple her adversary, England declared the whole coast of France, from Brest to the Elbe, in a state of blockade. The next year the English Government issued other orders in council, blockading the whole Continent, which were met by Napoleon's Milan decree. These famous orders in council, so far as they affected us, declared all American vessels going to and from the harbors of France and her allies, lawful prizes, except such as had at first touched at an English port, or allowed themselves to be searched by a British cruiser, the property of France, while British goods, wherever found, were subject to confiscation. In short, if we did not confine our commerce to England, the latter would seize our merchantmen wherever found, as lawful prizes; while, if we did trade with her, or even touch at her ports at all, France claimed them as her property."

Our men-of-war were compelled to look silently on and see American merchantmen seized, while both France and England claimed the right to plunder us. Our commerce for the last few years had advanced with unparalleled strides, so that at this time our canvas whitened almost every sea on the globe, and wealth was pouring into the nation. Suddenly, as if the whole world, without any forewarning, had declared war against us, the ocean was covered with cruisers after American vessels, and the commerce of the country was paralyzed by a single blow. These were the prominent causes of the war, sufficient, one would think, to justify the American Government in declaring it. One hundredth part of the provocation which we then endured, would now bring the two Governments in immediate and fierce collision. In 1794, Washington, in a letter to Mr. Jay, after speaking of the retention of posts which the British Government had, by treaty, ceded to us, and of the conduct of its agents in stirring up the Indians to hostilities, says: "Can it be expected, I ask, so long as these things are known in the United States, or, at least, firmly believed, and suffered with impunity by Great Britain, that there ever will or can be any cordiality between the two countries? I answer, No. And I will undertake, without the gift of prophecy, to predict that it will be impossible to keep this country in a state of amity with Great Britain long, if those posts are not surrendered." Still later, Jefferson, writing home from England, says: "In spite of treaties, England is our enemy. Her hatred is deep-rooted and cordial, and nothing with her is wanted but power to wipe us and the land we live in out of existence."

Notwithstanding all these insults and aggressions, the Government earnestly desired and sought to avoid a second conflict with England. The country had seen enough of war, and was beginning to feel anew the bounding pulse of returning health and prosperity. This hesitation emboldened the enemy, as our forbearance with the rebels at the beginning of the late revolt encouraged them, and the words and acts of contempt became the more bitter and undisguised. It is very striking that the immediate occasion of hostilities should forcibly remind us of more recent revelations of foreign aid in the conspiracy against the American Republic. Writes our great naval historian, Mr. Cooper: "In the winter of 1812, a plot on the part of English agents *to sever the American Union*, was revealed to the Government; and, at a later day, the determination of the English ministry to adhere to her orders in council, was formally communicated to the President. At the same time the claim to impress English seamen out of American ships on the high seas was maintained in theory, while in practice the outrage was constantly extended to natives; the boarding officers acting, in effect, on the unjust and perfectly illegal principle, that the seaman who failed to prove that he was an American, should be seized as an Englishman. Owing to these united causes, Congress formally declared war against the king of Great Britain, on the 18th of June, 1812.

"At the moment when this important intelligence was made public, nearly all of the little American marine were either in port or were cruising in the immediate vicinity of the coast. But a single ship, the Wasp, eighteen guns, Captain Jones, was on foreign service, and she was on her return from Europe with despatches. It is, however, some proof that the Government expected nothing more from its navy than a few isolated exploits that could produce no great influence on the main results of the contest, that the force the country actually possessed was not collected and ordered to act in a body during the short period that it would possess the advantage of assailing the enemy, while the latter was ignorant of the existence of hostilities. A squadron of three twenty-four-pounder frigates, of as many eighteen-pounder vessels of the same class, and of eight or ten smaller cruisers, all effective, well manned, and admirably officered, might have been assembled with a due attention to preparation. The enemy had but one two-decker, an old sixty-four, on the American coast, and the force just mentioned was quite sufficient to have blockaded both Halifax and Bermuda for a month, or until the English received intelligence of the war, and had time to reënforce from the West Indies. But the declaration of war did not find the little marine of America in a condition to act in a combined, intelligent, and military manner. The vessels were scattered, some were undergoing repairs, others were at a distance, and with the exception of one small squadron, every thing was virtually committed to the activity, judgment, and enterprise of the different captains. Information had been received of the sailing of a large fleet of Jamaica-men, under protection of a strong force, and these vessels would naturally be sweeping along the American coast, in the Gulf Stream. It was determined to make a dash at this convoy—as judicious a plan, under the circumstances, as could then have been adopted. Within an hour after he had received official information of the declaration of war, together with his orders, Commodore Rodgers, of the President, in New York harbor, was under way."

The squadron hearing, off Sandy Hook, June 21st, from an American vessel, that the Jamaica ships had been seen, crowded sail in pursuit. Soon the fast-sailing President shot ahead of the rest of the fleet, and at 4 o'clock P. M. was within gun range of the enemy. The wind then fell, giving the lighter Englishmen the advantage; and fearing they might get away, Commodore Rodgers determined to cripple them by opening fire. With his own hand he sent the first shot of the war intc a hostile ship. After a severe cannonade for three hours, during which the forecastle was blown up by a bursting gun, throwing Commodore Rodgers into the air, and breaking a leg in the fall, the contest was abandoned, because the Jamaica vessels kept too far ahead for the President's guns. Several men were killed on both sides—the baptism of blood upon the naval arena of warfare with haughty, boastful England.

The war, which was to be fought largely upon the sea, was now fairly opened. Our war-ships began to move at different points along the coast. Among the frigates honored with an early and conspicuous part in the strife was the ESSEX; and as our hero spent two years of his early youth under her pennant, and that, too, during time of war, you will like to know something of her history. The Essex was launched in 1799. This vessel was a frigate of twenty-six guns, called long twelves, but before the war, in their places, she mounted thirty-two pound carronades; a short cannon designed to throw heavy projectiles for breaking in, rather than piercing a ship's side, or other object at which it is aimed, and so called from Carron in Scotland, where they were first made. She was the first American man-of-war to carry the flag of the service east of the Cape of Good Hope, and was commanded by the brave Preble. He was afterwards commodore, as was his successor in the command of the Essex, the gallant Bainbridge, under whom the Essex shared in the Tripolitan war. When the President sailed, the Essex was lying in the harbor of New York.

The Constitution, of forty-four guns, Captain Hull, had gone to the Chesapeake, and soon after had her splendid and famous chase with the English fleet, of which the leading vessels were the Guerriere and Shannon.

CHAPTER V.

The Essex on the Ocean-plain of Conflict—A Prize—Midshipman Farragut—A Battle and a Victory—Naval Operations in other Quarters—The Essex ordered on a long Cruise—The Preparation—At Sea again.

SOON after Commodore Rodgers found the English fleet, Captain Porter left his moorings in New York for a *prize hunt* to the southward of the Grand Banks. How proudly, gladly, the ship's crew gazed upward to the national ensign, and out upon the wide and watery plain of conflict with the most powerful navy in the world! No hearts beat with wilder enthusiasm than those of the "middies;" and of this company of "young gentlemen," David G. Farragut, then eleven years of age, had no superior in manly, heroic spirit, panting to meet the enemy. See how closely the horizon is scanned for a sail spread over a hostile deck, or, at least, a lawful prize! At length one is visible, and the helm is turned to keep the prow toward the stranger. The Essex cuts the blue waters, sweeping down upon the unarmed trader. The summons to surrender rings out on the air, and the sight of the grim ordnance enforces the demand. A few moments later the captured craft, if not worth the trouble of keeping, is in flames, the crew prisoners of war, and again the frigate goes before the wind in search of another prize, until several have been taken, and the most of them left in charred fragments upon the waves. This was in July, 1812. A change in the weather drove the Essex northward, where for weeks she sought her foe.

At length the monotonous and tiresome scenes of fruitless search were changed. The clear soft night of early autumn was lit up with a "dull moon." The Essex floated upon the tide bathed in the "misty beams," which were reflected from the canvas tips of the rigging and the waters. It was a beautiful midnight scene. The "middies" were in their hammocks, and no signs of strife in the elements or among the crew were visible. Nature seemed reposing upon the bosom of infinite love. The watch was set, and scanned in vain the horizon's rim. The bells had softly proclaimed the morning, when there was a sudden start of interest among the wakeful few on the good ship. "Sail ho!" were the joyful words spoken with the animation that tells of the electric thrill which the prospect of a "lively time" sends through the heart of the mariner, among the silent cannon that girdle the deck of a man-of-war. An

English fleet was marching over the dim sea northward, and the same wind which filled its sails bore toward it the Essex, impatient to reach the unsuspecting enemy. Upon approaching the fleet, it was seen that "the English were sailing in very open order, with considerable intervals between them, and that the convoying ship, a large vessel, was some distance ahead, and, of course, to the leeward." The *convoy* is an armed ship for the protection of the vessels which it attends. The *leeward* is that direction toward which the wind blows. This position of the fleet decided Captain Porter to disguise the frigate, and reach the "sternmost ship of the strangers," to ascertain who they were, without exciting suspicion. The men of the Essex were at their guns, and every thing was ready for a fight. The morning had yet scarcely flushed the east, but there were now no sleepers on board. Every sailor-boy was at his post, but all whose presence would intimate the character of the cruiser were concealed, and their lower ports in. Soon the American frigate spoke the first ship, and Captain Porter learned that the fleet consisted of a few transports accompanied by a frigate and bomb-vessel. He then determined to get alongside of the British frigate, and get possession of her by surprise. Shooting ahead, the Essex came up to another transport and had further conversation, which so far awakened alarm, that the officer in command declared his intention to signal to the convoy that a stranger had joined the fleet. Disguise was no longer advisable, and throwing it aside, Captain Porter gave the Englishman to understand that silence and retiring from company to follow him, would alone save her from the metal of his carronades. All this was so quietly done that the prize was secured without exciting suspicion of what was transpiring in the rest of the fleet. The captured vessel contained one hundred and fifty troops. Before these could be removed and secured, the morning light rendered the designed attack on the convoy too doubtful an experiment to be attempted. This terminated the exciting moonlight chase, the first after a fleet with armed vessels, which had enlivened the decks of the Essex, and given a fair prospect to the "middies" of smelling powder.

A few days later the frigate discovered "a strange sail to the windward." The Essex was again concealed by a disguise. Her appearance was that of an unoffending merchantman on her way to some commercial port. Her gun-deck ports were in, "the topgallant masts housed, and the sails trimmed in a slovenly manner." Completely deceived by the harmless aspect of the stranger, the English ship sailed before the wind without a sign of fear, and consequently of preparation. Captain Porter, upon her approach, showed his ensign and kept out of his pursuer's way. This affected alarm emboldened the enemy, who, setting British colors, opened fire. It was now the turn of the Essex to show herself. The ports were cleared, and her carronades replied to the ordnance of England. What a moment was that to the midshipman who had never before even witnessed a naval engagement! The frigate trembles to the discharge of her thirty-two pounders, and their smoke curls upward toward the streaming pennant. After the second broadside, the Englishmen deserted their guns and ran below. In eight minutes after the Essex fired the enemy struck, and Captain Porter sent Lieutenant Finch on board to take possession of her. The prize was His Britannic Majesty's ship Alert, mounting twenty eighteen-pounder carronades. Although the Alert was inferior in armament to the Essex, this *first* capture of a man-of-war since hostilities commenced, wounded the pride of England, and encouraged this country, because it showed to both that the boasted and arrogant claim of the mother country to supremacy on the seas, might be an *exaggerated* impression, after all. Finding that the large number of prisoners taken contemplated mutiny in case another engagement afforded the opportunity, Captain Porter succeeded in making an arrangement with the commanding officer of the Alert, to send the frigate as a cartel to St. John's; *i. e.* a ship of truce, carrying prisoners or despatches, and exempt from capture. Continuing her cruise southward of the Grand Banks, the Essex fell in with hostile frigates, and repeated the almost successful game with the convoy a short time before. Having done nobly in her first cruise of the war, she returned to moorings in the Delaware to get fresh supplies, and await further orders from the Government. The weeks in port passed swiftly by; the officers and crew visiting the shore, and sharing in the social life and change of scene, the seamen for awhile so intensely enjoy. The longing for active service, however, returns, and the orders to prepare for a voyage again was hailed by the people of the Essex. The fresh start for distant seas I will give you in the words of the brave commander's journal, in which will be found the name of DAVID G. FARRAGUT. I shall quote the names of the officers only, down to the "Boy;" and from the record of the voyage, to the *first bird*. Writes Captain Porter:

"*October* 6, 1812.—I received orders from Commodore William Bainbridge to prepare the Essex for a long cruise, and on the day following received his final instructions, appointing places of rendezvous, and the next day a copy of his orders from the honorable Secretary of the Navy.

"I consequently directed the ship to be furnished with every requisite supply of stores, etc.; ordered for her a new suit of sails and standing rigging; took out the bowsprit and fished it, and put her in the best possible state for service, taking in as much provisions as she could stow, and providing ourselves with a double supply of clothing, and fruit, vegetables, and lime juice as antiscorbutics. I also gave the officers and men intimation of the probable length of our cruise, in order that they might supply themselves with such comforts as their means would admit of, they having recently been paid a proportion of the prize-money for the last cruise, and advanced the officers three months' pay. They accordingly furnished themselves with stock, vegetables, and other stores, in as large quantities as could be stowed away, and on the afternoon of the 28th we left the Capes of Delaware, with the wind from the northward, which gradually hauled around to the westward, blowing fresh, with thick weather, so that it was with difficulty we were enabled to weather the dangerous shoals of Chincoteague.

"Prior to the pilot's leaving us, I caused him to deliver into my possession all letters which might have been given him by the crew, apprehensive that, from some accidental cause, they might have become possessed of a knowledge of our destination. They all, however, contained only conjectures, except one, the writer of which asserted, as he stated, from good authority, that we were bound on the coast of Africa. As some of their conjectures were not far from being correct, I thought it best to destroy the whole of them, and forbid the pilot's taking any more without my consent. To the officers who were desirous of writing to their friends, I enjoined particularly not to mention the movements of the ship in any way.

"On the morning of the 29th, the wind hauled around

to the westward, and increased to a gale. Got the ship under snug sail, and secured our masts, by setting up the rigging, which being new, had stretched considerably. The ship being very deep, we found her unusually laborsome and uncomfortable; her straining, occasioned by her deep rolling, opened her water-ways, and kept the berth-deck full of water, damaged a great deal of our provisions stowed on it, and wet all the bedding and clothes of the crew; found also the coal-hole full of water; found a leak somewhere between the cutwater and stem, but in other respects the ship was tight; for, after scuttling the berth-deck and bulkhead of the coal-hole, we could easily keep her free by pumping a few minutes every two hours.

"Previous to leaving the river the crew had been put on allowance of half a gallon of water each man per day; and being desirous of making our provisions hold out as long as possible, having views, at the same time, with regard to the health of the crew, I caused the allowance of bread to be reduced one-half, and issued, in lieu of the remainder, half a pound of potatoes, or the same quantity of apples. Every other article of provisions was reduced one-third, excepting rum, of which the full allowance was served out raw to the cook of each mess (the crew being divided into messes of eight, and a cook allowed to each), who was accountable for its faithful distribution. For the undrawn provisions, the purser's steward was directed to issue due-bills, with assurances on my part that they should be paid the amount on our arrival in port. Orders were given to lose no opportunity of catching rain-water for the stock, of which we had a large quantity on board, every mess in the ship being supplied with pigs and poultry. The allowance of candles was reduced one-half, and economy established respecting the consumption of wood and the expenditure of the ship's stores. Habits of cleanliness and care with respect to clothing were strongly recommended to the officers and crew. I now gave a general pardon for all offences committed on board; recommended the strictest attention to the discipline of the ship; held out prospects of reward to those who should be vigilant in the performance of their duty, and gave assurances that the first man I was under the necessity of punishing should receive three dozen lashes; expressing a hope, however, that punishment during the cruise would be altogether unnecessary. I directed, as a standing regulation, that the ship should be fumigated in every part every morning, by pouring vinegar on a red-hot shot, and confided to Lieutenant Finch the superintendence of the berth-deck, in order to preserve it in a cleanly and wholesome state. Lime being provided in tight casks, for the purpose of white-washing, and sand for dry-rubbing it, and orders given not to wet it if there should be a possibility of avoiding it, a comfortable place was fitted up for the accommodation of the sick on the berth-deck; cleets were put up for slinging as many hammocks as possible on the gun-deck; and orders given that no wet clothes or wet provisions should be permitted to remain on the berth-deck, nor the crew be permitted to eat anywhere but on the gun-deck, except in bad weather. Having established the above and other regulations as regarded the health and comfort of the crew, I exhorted the officers to keep them occupied constantly during working hours in some useful employment, and directed that two hours between four and six o'clock in the afternoon, should be allowed to them for amusement, when the duties of the ship would admit.

"The 30th was devoted entirely to airing the bedding, drying the clothing of the crew that was wet during the gale, getting the berth-deck in the most comfortable state, exercising the crew at the great guns, and putting the ship in the best state for service. We found the powder in several of our guns wet, all of which we reloaded, and more carefully secured.

"Previous to leaving the Delaware we landed at the hospital those men whose health I did not conceive would enable them to stand the fatigues of the cruise. As they had most of them been a long time on the surgeon's list, and were considered incurable, I believed it advisable not to take them to sea.

"My crew at the time of my departure consisted of the following persons:

No.	*Names.*	*Rank.*
2.	John Downes	1st Lieutenant.
3.	James P. Wilmer	2d "
4.	James Wilson	3d "
5.	William Finch	Acting 4th Lieut.
6.	Stephen D. M'Knight	" 5th "
7.	John G. Cowell	Sailing-master.
8.	Robert Miller	Surgeon.
9.	David P. Adams	Chaplain.
10.	John R. Shaw	Purser.
11.	William H. Haddiway	Midshipman.
12.	David G. Farragut	"
13.	Richard Dashiell	"
14.	John S. Cowan	"
15.	Charles T. Clark	"
16.	William H. Odenheimer	"
17.	Henry W. Ogden	"
18.	Henry Gray	"
19.	George W. Isaacs	"
20.	William W. Feltus	"
21.	Thomas A. Conover	"
22.	David Tittermary	"
23.	Richard K. Hoffman	Acting Sur. mate.
24.	Alexander M. Montgomery	"
25.	Edward Linscott	Boatswain.
26.	Lawrence Miller	Gunner.
27.	John S. Waters	Carpenter.
28.	David Navarro	Sailmaker.
29.	W. W. Bostwick	Captain's clerk.
30.	William P. Pierce	Master's mate.
31.	James Terry	"

No.	Names.	Rank.
32.	Thomas Belcher	Boatswain's mate.
33.	Joseph Hawley	"
34.	William Kingsbury	"
35.	George Martin	Gunner's mate.
36.	James Spafford	"
37.	John Langley	Carpenter's mate.
38.	Bennet Field	Armorer.
39.	George Kensinger, jr.	Master-at-arms.
40.	John Adams	Cooper.
41.	John Francis	Coxswain.
42.	Thomas Coleman	Steward.
43.	John Haden	Cook.
44.	Thomas Bailey	Boatswain's yeom'n.
45.	Thomas Edwards	Gunner's yeoman.
46.	Benjamin Wodden	Carpenter's yeoman.
47.	James Rynard	Quartermaster.
48.	Francis Bland	"
49.	William Gardner	"
50.	John Mallet	"
51.	Robert Dunn	"
52.	John Thompson	"
53.	Isaac Valance	"
54.	Benjamin Geers	Quarter-gunner.
55.	Adam Roach	"
56.	James Steady	"
57.	Leonard Green	"
58.	James Marshall	"
59.	Edwin Sellman	"
60.	Henry Stone	"
61.	Henry Ruff	Boy.

RECAPITULATION.

1	Captain,	1	Master-at-arms,
5	Lieutenants,	1	Steward,
1	Lieutenant of Marines,	1	Coxswain,
1	Sailing-master,	1	Cooper,
1	Chaplain,	1	Cook,
1	Purser,	1	Boatswain's yeoman,
1	Surgeon,	1	Gunner's yeoman,
2	Surgeon's mates,	1	Carpenter's yeoman,
12	Midshipmen,	7	Quartermasters,
1	Boatswain,	7	Quarter-gunners,
1	Gunner,	2	Sergeants,
1	Carpenter,	2	Corporals,
1	Sailmaker,	1	Drummer,
1	Captain's clerk,	1	Fifer,
2	Master's mates,	25	Private marines,
3	Boatswain's mates,	227	Seamen, ordinary seamen, landsmen, boys, and supernumeraries.
2	Gunner's mates,		
1	Carpenter's mate,		
1	Armorer,	319	Total

"On the 2d of November the weather began to grow more moderate, in consequence of which we got up from below all the bread and vegetables stowed on the berth-deck, for the purpose of separating the damaged from the rest. Found about four barrels of bread entirely spoiled, and the same quantity of apples. All the barrels were wet; we therefore started the whole of them, dried the provisions, repacked and stowed them away to more advantage, securing them against further damage from leaks by covering them with tarpaulins; also, cut two scuttles in the berth-deck to carry off such water as might enter by the leaks in the waterways, stem, and down the hatchways; also, took advantage of the good weather to fleet and set up our main rigging, to render the masts more secure; unbent the fore-topsail, which was injured by chafing, and bent another.

"Having had favorable winds since our departure, we this day found ourselves in the latitude of 36° 7′ north; longitude, by dead reckoning, 58° 54′ west; but with a view of getting into a latitude where we might expect more moderate weather, as well as to cross the track of vessels bound from England to Bermudas, and those from the West Indies to Europe, stood to the southeast.

"On the morning of the 3d a sail was discovered to the southwest; made all sail in chase, and at 8 o'clock discovered her to be a Portuguese merchant brig bound to the westward; gave over chase, and stood on to the southeast, with light winds from the north and variable; sent up our royalmasts, and employed the crew in various useful jobs, the sick and cooks of the messes being occupied in picking oakum for caulking the waterways, which were found to be very open, in consequence of the oakum having washed out. Got up the marine clothing from the store-room to air, as some of it was found to be wet from the leak in the stem; the other store-rooms on examination proved to be dry. Also, employed the sailmakers in repairing the fore-topsail that was unbent, and gave directions to the officers to get their boats in the best state for service (each lieutenant of the ship, as well as the sailing-master, having charge of one). Toward the latter part of the day the wind hauled around from the eastward, and threatened rain. This day saw a bird that very much resembled a plover in appearance and note."

How full of interest this glimpse of the Essex with her 320 souls, pushing out upon the faithless, pathless ocean, to encounter not only its ordinary perils, but the wrath of an enemy, whose powerful navy was anticipating a speedy conquest of the fleets of the new Republic! It was no "elegant leisure" for officers or men, as the "getting off" has clearly shown. I wish we knew more of the emotions, and words, and deeds of Midshipman Farragut. But neither he nor his friends on shipboard anticipated a day when the very prattle of his childhood would have an interest to grateful, admiring millions. This we do know, that with a daring and enthusiasm beyond his years, he entered into all the duties and exciting scenes of a mariner's career, commenced almost at the moment when battle-flags fluttered over the canvas of English and American ships.

CHAPTER VI.

On to Port Praya—Its Position and People—Incidents interesting to the "Young Gentlemen"—The Sleeping Apartments on board a Frigate—Captain Porter cares for his People—Encounter with a British Brig—The Prize—At St. Catharine's.

NOVEMBER 3d, you will recollect, the Essex made the first chase of the cruise—an exciting change in the pleasant voyage. Sunshine and showers — gentle winds and calms — succeeded each other; the "young gentlemen" enjoying the really delightful nautical scenery which on the evening of the 5th was remarkably beautiful. As twilight came on, the clouds floated around the horizon in fantastic forms, variegated with gorgeous and delicate hues, till every eye was attracted to the enchanting view. A light breeze swelled the new canvas, which, with the serene and richly-bordered sky, was reflected from the gently-undulating ocean. Commodore Porter alludes to the evening with enthusiastic admiration.

The next day was more breezy, and the frigate marched

over the waves under a glorious sky, with nothing to interrupt the usual round of duty. "At night a magnificent meteor shot out upon the clear sky, and continued to glitter several minutes before it exploded."

Upon the 7th "Sail ho! sail ho!" comes from the lips of the watcher for the welcome sight; and soon the warlike aspect of the distant ship is visible. The men spring to their posts, and the chase begins. The hours of day vanish, and still the Essex spreads all her sails in the pursuit of the stranger. How unlike the evening before! Now all thought is turned to the flying ship, which eludes the Essex under the cover of darkness.

The sick list of the frigate decreased daily, because of the excellent sanitary arrangements of the thoughtful, benevolent commander. The name of Farragut nowhere appears on the roll of the invalids, his correct manner of life saving him from the dreaded solitude of sickness.

On the moonlight evening of the 16th, the appreciative eye of the young midshipman was charmed with a scene not uncommon in this latitude; every object in view wore a *green* hue. The atmosphere seemed to glow with an emerald light, bathing sky and sea. The softness and loveliness of the horizon, and of the ocean, whose bosom at that hour was fanned by the light breath of Nature sinking into repose, cannot be imagined by one who has not beheld it.

The next morning brought another stir among the

men of the Essex. The day was calm, and while giving "the rigging a good setting-up" a sail was discerned in the distance, and the frigate in a few moments was steering directly for it. The chase was short, the vessel proving to be a Portuguese brig, and bringing the news of embargo laid upon American vessels in the Brazils upon hearing of the war.

Scarcely was the chase over before the sea-world again put on the emerald glory of her tropical enchantment, attracting all eyes to the suggestive contrast with the rising conflict between two Christian nations.

November 23d the Essex approached the tropics off the coast of North America, and her decks became the scene of all sorts of comedy—it was the sailor's ceremony of "crossing the line." Old Neptune was represented with his train of imps, barbers, etc., the "middies" sharing in the strange and varied entertainment.

Wrote the indulgent commander: "Neptune, however, and most of his suite, paid their devotions so frequently to Bacchus, that before the christening was half gone through, their godships were unable to stand; the business was therefore entrusted to subordinates, who performed both the shaving and washing with as little regard to tenderness as his majesty would have done.

"On the whole, they got through the business with less disorder and more good humor than I expected; and though some were most unmercifully scratched, the only satisfaction sought was that of shaving others in their turn with newly-invented tortures."

Scarcely had the crew sobered down before Midshipman Farragut looked upon two green islands, between which the frigate lay, with all the interest of ardent boyhood, far out at sea, amid novel, strange, and often inspiring scenes. His commander and friend will tell you what he saw; and who would not like to have shared with him the luscious fruits?

"On the morning of the 27th we were between the isles of Mayo and St. Jago. On the sides of the mountains of the latter we could perceive several villages and large flocks of goats, but the arid appearance of the soil scarcely left us the hope that it would afford us the refreshments we required, as no vegetable or tree of any description could be perceived by us, except a few scattering cocoa-nut trees. The island had altogether a most dreary and uncultivated appearance, and I had partly determined in my own mind only to look into the road of Praya, to see if there were any of our ships of war there, as this was the first rendezvous fixed on by Commodore Bainbridge. At 2 P. M. rounded to the east point of Porto Praya, and stretched into the harbor, showing the American colors, the Portuguese being displayed on a flashy flagstaff erected on a hill at one corner of the ruins of a fort in the bottom of the bay, and in front of the town. Perceiving no vessels in the bay except a small

Portuguese schooner, I hauled off; but being desirous of procuring some information respecting the Commodore, as this was the day appointed by him to leave this place for Fernando de Noronha, I concluded on sending Lieutenant Downes ashore with a person who could speak the Portuguese language; and as a pretext for so doing, I directed him to state to the governor that we were an American frigate wanting supplies, to request his permission to obtain them, to inform him I should fire a salute provided he would return gun for gun, and that I should, provided I anchored, take the earnest opportunity of making my respects to him. On the return of Mr. Downes he informed me that the governor could not be seen, as he had gone to take his afternoon nap, but that the lieutenant-governor, or second in command, informed him we could obtain every supply we stood in need of; that the salute should be returned gun for gun; that the governor would be happy to see me on shore; expressed his astonishment that I should have asked permission to come in; and concluded with an offer of his services in procuring the supplies we might want. Mr. Downes informed me that no government vessels of war had been at Praya; that the American privateer Yankee, from Boston, and another privateer from Salem, and an armed British schooner, had been there not long since. I consequently concluded to stop a few days; and during the time to fill up our water and take in refreshments. I therefore ran in and anchored in seven fathoms of water, clear sandy bottom, the flagstaff bearing N.N.W., and the east end of Quail Island west by compass. We fired the salute, which was punctually returned.

"At nine o'clock on the morning of the 28th I waited on his excellency, accompanied by some of the officers. He was engaged at the time on some business at the custom-house, as I was informed, and could not be seen until about eleven; the second in command, however, Major Medina, who spoke indifferent English, entertained us during the interval, making offers of his services in procuring the supplies, of which we gave him a list. After making the necessary arrangements and fixing on the prices, we waited on the governor, whom we found at his house, dressed in all his splendor to receive us. His reception was of the most friendly nature, and I am persuaded he was much pleased to see us in the port. He expressed much regret that the war had deprived them of the advantage arising from the American commerce, as they had been cut off from all their supplies, and were now destitute of bread and every other comfort of life except what the island afforded, which consisted chiefly in live stock and fruit. He told me that a little flour, or any thing else we could spare, would be most acceptable to him, and invited me to make my dinner with him, on such scanty fare as he was enabled to give me; adding, if I would come on shore next day, he would endeavor to provide something better. I accepted his invitation with as little ceremony as it was given; and although there was but little variety of meats, he had an abundant supply of the best tropical fruits I ever tasted. The oranges were very fine. We this day commenced watering; but, after having to roll the casks about five hundred yards, found great difficulty in getting them from the beach, on account of the heavy surf.

"On the 29th I again dined with the governor, and from that time until the morning of the 2d of December, we were occupied in getting on board refreshments and water; but of the latter we were only enabled to get about five thousand gallons. The beef was very dear, and very poor; a bullock weighing three hundred weight cost thirty-five dollars; sheep were three dollars, but very poor, oranges forty cents per hundred, and other fruits in the same proportion and in the greatest abundance. It is supposed that the ship had not on board less than one hundred thousand oranges, together with a large quantity of cocoa-nuts, plantains, lemons, limes, casada, etc. Every mess on board were also supplied with pigs, sheep, fowls, turkeys, goats, etc., which were purchased tolerably cheap; fowls at three dollars per dozen, and fine turkeys at one dollar each; many of the seamen, also, furnished themselves with monkeys and young goats as pets, and when we sailed from thence the ship bore no slight resemblance, as respected the different animals on board her, to Noah's ark.

"In the town of Praya there are not more than thirty whites; the rest of the population is made up of slaves and free negroes, making altogether not more than three thousand, of whom about four hundred are soldiers. All the officers, except three or four, are mulattoes, and their priest is a negro, who possesses considerable polish of manners. The soldiers are generally destitute of clothing from the waist upward; and it can be asserted with a certainty of adhering strictly to the truth, that there are not five serviceable muskets in Praya. Most of them are without any locks, their stocks broken off at the breech, their barrels tied into the stocks with a leather thong, or a cord made of the fibres of the cocoa-nut; and it was no uncommon thing to see a naked negro mounting guard, shouldering a musket barrel only. Their cavalry were in a corresponding style, mounted on jackasses, and armed with broken swords. The governor informed me it had been ten years since they had received any pay, or supplies of clothing or arms.

"The guns of different calibres mounted about Praya, for the defence of the place, although in commanding situations, are in a state equally bad with the muskets of the negroes. They are placed on ship's carriages, which are old and rotten, scarcely holding together, without platform, shelter, or breastwork, except a slight dilapidated one before the saluting battery, and another in as bad a state on the west point of the bay. The whole number of guns amounts to thirty; and for them chiefly they are indebted to a Portuguese frigate that was lost by the negligence of her officers about three years since. Porto Praya could be taken, and every gun spiked, by thirty men.

"An abundance of fish may be caught with the hook and line alongside, and with the seine on the beach, where we hauled every morning during our stay—one afternoon at the particular request of the governor, when himself and the ladies of his family, as well as all the other white ladies of the town, consisting altogether of seven, besides the white and colored officers, attended. We were not at that time so fortunate as we were afterwards; we however caught enough to afford them a mess, which I caused to be carried to their houses. A very good amusement may be had in the bay by rowing with a small boat across the mouth, and towing a line with a hook fastened on with wire, and baited with small fish, for the purpose of catching barracoutas. The best time is in the dusk of the evening and at daylight in the morning.

"On the 29th, after dinner, the governor visited the ship, with the ladies of his family and all the officers of the garrison, black and white; on his leaving us I caused a salute of eleven guns to be fired. He was much pleased with the attentions paid him, and next day spoke of it with renewed offers of civility. I sent him, as well as Medina, a barrel of flour and pork, with some other small articles, and in return he sent me off six fine turkeys. From the favorable disposition of the governor and officers of the government, as well as the facility of procuring refreshments, I would recommend Port Praya as an excellent place for our ships to stop for supplies. The bay is of easy access, and when the anchor is once settled in the bottom, is perfectly safe. It is necessary, however, to give the ship half a cable before you check her, or the anchor is not likely to take hold, and there is danger of her going on the rocks of Quail Island, as was the case with the Portuguese frigate.

"As the governor hinted to me that a letter from me to our minister at the court of Brazil would be agreeable to him, I wrote such a one as I thought would be flattering to him, and sent it on shore, informing him of my intentions to sail that day. A signal was in consequence hoisted (as he informed my officer) to *permit* us to depart.

"The governor is about forty-five years of age, a man of easy and agreeable manners and friendly disposition. The utmost respect is paid to him by all subject to his authority. No one is ever seated in his presence; and, whenever he leaves his quarters, he is always accompanied by a guard; when on foot, he is preceded by a soldier bearing a halbert.

"The friendly attentions we met with in the port of Praya could not have been exceeded in any port of the United States; and as the Portuguese are the allies of Great Britain, their attentions were as surprising as they were unexpected. I found, however, after I had been with them a short time, that their attachments to the Americans, growing out of their commercial interests and concerns, were very strong; that the only British vessels that ever touched there were vessels of war, who came for supplies, with the haughty unconciliating conduct of the commanders and officers, of which they were by no means satisfied. They spoke of the prince regent as the slave, the tool of the British Government, and were highly gratified with the accounts I gave them of our little success over the ships of that imperious navy. The governor assured me he would give me *every protection* against *any British force* that should arrive there during my stay, and expressed a strong desire that we should make him another visit, when he hoped to make our time more agreeable.

"The two greatest evils to guard against in refreshing at Porto Praya, is the bad rum of the country and the heat of the sun, to both of which the watering party are unavoidably exposed. The negroes and seamen have such a variety of expedients for getting rum on board, that it is almost impossible to detect them. They hover about the beach with the bottles under their arms, where the shawls of the females serve the better to conceal them; and at a favorable opportunity they bury them in the sand, receive their money, while the sailor watches his opportunity for getting it on board or drinking it. They sometimes draw the milk from the cocoa-nuts, fill them with rum, and sell them to the seamen in that state at a high price. The first day we were employed in watering we had several men drunk; but after that we were more fortunate, as I selected the most trusty men to fill and roll the casks to the beach, with directions to make a signal when they were ready to tow off. By this means we prevented our boats' crews from having any communication with the shore. A similar precaution was used in getting our supplies of fruit on board: they were brought to the beach by the negroes, and, on a signal being made, boats were sent for them. I should advise ships that intend getting any considerable supplies of water, to employ negroes altogether for filling the casks and rolling them down to the beach, as it would entirely prevent the necessity of exposing the men either to the inclemency of the sun or the temptations held out to them. The watering-place is a well at the back of the town, in a valley, and the only place from whence the inhabitants receive their supply.

"On the day of our departure there were nine patients, three from accidents and three with inflammatory bilious fevers. This was one cause of my hastening from thence before I had completed filling my water, as I was fearful of introducing disease among the crew. None of the last selected watering-party on shore were in the slightest degree affected by the climate, although employed from daylight in the morning until late at night. They were, however, shaded a considerable part of the time by the groves of cocoa-nut trees that grow between the landing-place and the well, and they were not compelled to work in the middle of the day; added to this, those employed after the first day were very temperate, and not known to enter into any excesses.

"Praya may be known by an old fort on Point Tubaron; by the black island of Quails, on which several guns are mounted; by the fort and town of Praya; and by a flagstaff, or signal establishment, situated on a mountain at the back of the east point of the bay. Praya is situated on a plain, on the top of a rock overlooking the bay, the sides of which, toward the sea, are everywhere nearly perpendicular, rendering all approaches impracticable except by two roads, one on the east, the other on the west, which have been cut in the rock, and are very steep. The houses, or cabins, except those of the principal officers, are built of rough stone, one story high, and covered with the branches of the cocoa-nut tree. The police of Praya is rigid, no one is permitted to wear concealed weapons; and had I not been well assured that there were no better arms in the island, I should have supposed that fears of an insurrection induced them to put unserviceable muskets and broken cutlasses into the hands of their naked negro soldiers."

December 3d, "Levi Holmes departed this life. His remains were committed to the deep, according to the funeral ceremonies of the church."

What a touching episode in the history of the Essex is this brief record! A burial at sea! The crew are summoned to the deck, the body of the dead mariner is in its sack with weights attached; and when the solemn words are uttered, "Earth to earth—dust to dust," the shroud and coffin, with its human form, glides into the sea, and rapidly disappears till it becomes a white speck, and then is lost to sight forever! The health of the more than three hundred people of the frigate was remarkably good; and the reason for it you will learn from another passage of Captain Porter's journal:

"My chief care was now the health of my people; and all the means that suggested themselves to my mind to effect this great object were adopted. The utmost cleanliness was required from every person on board, and directions were given for mustering the crew every morning at their quarters, where they were strictly examined by their officers. It was recommended to them to bathe at least once a day, and the officers were requested to show them the example. They were required, also, to use every means in their power to provide constant employment for the men under their control during working hours, and amusement for them during the hours of recreation, and to be particularly careful not to harass them by disturbing them unnecessarily during their watch below, as also to guard against any improper or unnecessary exposure to the weather. Economy was recommended to the crew in the use of their supply of fruit, and permission was given to suspend it in the rigging and other airy parts of the ship, in nets made for the purpose, with a promise of the severest punishment to such as should be detected in stealing from others. With those precautions to procure exercise and cleanliness, with proper ventilations and fumigations, a young, active, healthy, and contented crew, a ship in good order for the service we were engaged in, well found with the best provisions and the purest water, perfectly free from all bad taste and smell, I do not conceive why we should be in greater apprehension of disease originating on board now, than on the coast of North America. We have friendly ports under our lee, where we may stop from time to time to procure the necessary supplies of refreshments; and the weather has not been oppressive, but a moderate and steady breeze from the east contributed greatly to refresh the air; and sailing could not be more pleasant than our passage toward the line. The landsmen on board were delighted with it, and the seamen felicitated themselves that it was *not always the case at sea*, 'or all the old women in the country would have been sailors.' The animals on board becoming a serious burden on account of water, the commander ordered them to be killed, notwithstanding the seamen begged for the life of a favorite kid, or pig, designed for Christmas."

Besides the arrangements to secure health on board the Essex, already given, the crew were permitted to sleep on the *gun-deck*. This is the large deck where the cannon are handled, having the ports for their muzzles, which admit of a fine circulation of fresh air—a spacious, well-ventilated apartment. But most of the commanders have been opposed to the indulgence, because the hammocks were in the way of the guns if suddenly needed for an enemy.

In the language of the humane Porter, "what can be more dreadful than for three hundred men to be confined with their hammocks, being only eighteen inches apart on the berth-deck of a small frigate, a space of seventy feet long, thirty-five wide, and five high, in a hot climate, where the only apertures by which they can receive air are two hatchways of about six feet square? A call to their watch must be a relief from their sufferings; and although it exposes them to all the ills attending the violent and sudden chills occasioned by the dews and night air while the pores are open, and the body in a profuse perspiration, it is more tolerable than suffocation. Those sudden and frequent changes from heat to cold must, in time, wear out the strongest constitution, and produce incurable diseases. From the number confined in so small a space, the whole atmosphere of the ship becomes tainted, and not only those who are compelled to sleep below, but every person on board, is affected by the pernicious vapors arising from the berth-deck."

And the brave, amiable sovereign of the Essex answers like a hero who knows how to manage war-ships and men, the objection of inconvenience in mustering the force for battle. He says, that by using the gun-deck for a dormitory, he has the advantage of "always having the men near their quarters, where, on the slightest alarm, they may be ready for action. Should circumstances make it necessary for us to pipe up the hammocks on seeing a strange sail at night, they can be lashed up much sooner and with less confusion on a roomy gun-deck, than from a dark and crowded berth-deck. But if it should happen (which cannot be the case with a good lookout) that a vessel is close on board before she is discovered, and there should not be time to get the hammocks on deck, it is an easy matter to cut away the lanyards, and throw the hammocks below, or on one side, clear of the guns. They are compelled to sling the hammocks opposite their guns, and are accountable for the safety of every article belonging to them. Ships that adopt this regulation, with other proper precautions, have always healthy crews; and this circumstance alone, which contributes so much to their comfort, and in time of action must render them more efficient, should overcome the trifling, ill-founded apprehension of not having the hammocks stowed in time for action. Fifteen minutes are sufficient at any time to make every preparation for action; and on discovering a vessel at night, there can be no circumstance which should render it necessary to run alongside of her without taking that much time to prepare for battle. In order to have the hammocks in a greater state of readiness for stowing away, orders were given that every man, on turning out to take his watch, should lash his hammock up in readiness to take on deck.

"The sick are never permitted to remain on the gun-deck at night, but are brought up by their messmates every morning, and their hammocks are slung in some cool, agreeable part of the gun-deck, where they will not be disturbed by persons at work or running against them."

December 11th the Essex crossed the equator, that invisible and central line girdling the globe, of which a sailor affirmed that he felt the *jar* when the vessel went over it.

The next day, after noon, the watchman again cries, "A sail, ho!" The ship looks like an English brig-of-war, and all hands prepare for the chase. For four hours the frigate cuts the foam, gaining upon the strange craft. A signal on her mast decides her British character, and Captain Porter puts answering signals of a similar kind to decoy the enemy. The brig is deceived, and hoists her colors at sunset. This was the fifth vessel pursued since the cruise began. At nine o'clock the ships were within musket shot, and ordering the large guns not to be fired, to save the brig from injury as far as possible, Captain Porter demanded a surrender. Instead of doing this he tried to run athwart the stern of the Essex, give a raking fire, and escape. A volley of musketry brought the Englishman to terms. The same night $55,000, with the prisoners, were removed. And to show you farther, the influence under which the sailor-boy Farragut was trained thus early, moulding his character into that symmetrical, attractive, and elevated form it bears, I will let his commander, who was also a father to him, tell the rest of the story of the capture:

"On the 13th, despatched the prize under the command of Lieutenant Finch, and as I sent in her seventeen of the prisoners, I was under the necessity of parting with as many of my own crew. I put on board the prize the captain, master, and passengers; and, with a view of securing their neutrality in the event of any attempt to retake the vessel, I permitted them to go on parole of honor, with the privilege of embarking on board any vessel they might meet, bound to England or elsewhere. As I have never permitted prisoners to be plundered in any one instance, the officers and passengers of the brig soon felt themselves, while on board the Essex, at perfect ease, and secure from any violence; and they seemed to consider their capture and trip to America more in the light of an agreeable adventure, or party of pleasure, than a misfortune.

"A Mr. James Heyworth, a merchant from Brazils, on leaving my ship, presented me with two letters unsealed, which he requested me to present in the event of my going to Rio Janeiro. One of them I found to be a letter of introduction; the other announcing his capture. To show the sentiments by which he was impressed, I shall give a copy of them both.

"'December 12, 1812.

"'DEAR BROTHER LAWRENCE: By the extreme civility of the gentleman who offers to forward this, I am enabled to inform you that we have been captured by an American vessel. However, we are proceeding under the direction of a prize-master to the United States; have liberty, if we fall in with a neutral vessel, to go on on board; and if not, we shall proceed to North America. I am under my parole, and expect soon to be with my friends in England.

"'We have been most humanely treated. I cannot inform you more particulars, having given my word of honor not to disclose any thing relative to our capture.

I am well, thank God, in good spirits, and request you will make yourself easy respecting me.

"'I am, dear Lawrence,

"'Your affectionate brother,

"'JAMES HEYWORTH.

"'Los. Senrs. HEYWORTH, IRMOOS & Co.,
No. 10, *Resa das Violas*, *Rio de Janeiro*.'

"'AMERICAN FRIGATE ESSEX, AT SEA, December 13, 1812.

"'GENTLEMEN: Should it occur that the bearer of this letter, Captain Porter, commander of the United States frigate Essex, visits your port, I have to entreat of you that you will show him every civility and hospitality in your power.

"'By attending to this request you will essentially oblige me; and by doing which you cannot possibly return, in a suitable manner, the heavy obligations I lie under to Captain Porter, for his very generous and humane conduct to me whilst a prisoner on board his frigate.

"'I remain, dear sirs, very respectfully,

"'Your most obedient servant,

"'JAMES HEYWORTH.

"'Messrs. HEYWORTH, BROTHERS & Co., *Rio de Janeiro*.'

"The Nocton proving to be a beautiful vessel, and well calculated for the United States service, I took the liberty of recommending her to the Secretary of the Navy as a cruiser; being anxious that one of the enemy's small vessels should be taken into our service, to supply the place of the Nautilus, which had been taken by the British a short time before.

"The island Fernando de Noronha, which you will see on the map, off the Coast of Brazil, was the next object of unusual interest, rising like a dark spire from the ocean, and sometimes mistaken, as it was on board the Essex, for a ship in the distance. Here they anchored under disguise, and sent on shore to hear, if possible, from Commodore Bainbridge, whom it was expected to join in this latitude. He had been there and gone, but such was the intelligence gleaned, that Captain Porter thought he might yet find him. This island was a prison, indeed, well fortified in every part, and its population consisting of a few miserable, naked exiled Portuguese, and as miserable a guard. The governor is changed every three years, and during his term of service in the island has the privilege of disposing of its produce to his own emolument. Cattle in abundance, hogs, goats, fowls, etc., may be had there, as well as corn, melons, cocoa-nuts, etc. Ships, formerly, frequently touched for refreshments, wood, and water, but for seven months prior to the arrival of the Acasta, none had been there. There are no females on the island, and none are permitted to be there, from what motives I cannot conceive, except it be to render the place of exile the more horrible. The watering-place is near the beach, at the foot of the rock on which the citadel is placed, and it is with the utmost difficulty and danger that the casks can be got through the surf to the boat. There is no boat in the island, and the only means of communication between Wooding Island and Fernando, is a small raft of catamaran, which is carefully kept in one of the forts, and is capable of bearing only two men. An abundance of fish may be procured, with but little trouble, with the hook and line.

"As clothing is not in use here, as hunger may be gratified without labor, and as there is an appearance of cheerfulness, those that are not in chains may be supposed, in some measure, reconciled to a state as good, perhaps, as any they had formerly been accustomed to."

December 13th, "A sail, ho! A sail, ho!" is heard, for the first time since the Nocton was seized, and spread great excitement among the crew, already impatient for a chase and a battle. But the enemy's ship was sailing under Portuguese colors, and the Essex went on her way to escape recognition. After pursuing and taking the Elizabeth, starting off in an "uproar" of excitement after *small clouds*, mistaken for sails, the frigate dropped her anchor near the island of St. Catharine's, to replenish, if practicable, the exhausted refreshments. This prospect sent a new thrill of delight over the man-of-war, from captain to the "middies" not only, but to the humblest "supernumerary," who must have his ration of food and water, and I am sorry to add, in those days, of *rum* to madden his brain.

CHAPTER VII.

A Farewell to Moorings—Around Cape Horn—Scanty Fare—A Rat a Dainty—A Cup of Pure Water at Sea—Gales—Perils Doubling the Cape—Mocha—A Tragedy.

THE officers and men having provided themselves with pigs, fowls, plantains, yams, etc., prepared to set sail. Fresh beef which had spoiled on account of the heat, was thrown overboard, when a gigantic shark, twenty-five feet in length, rose to the surface with the "*quarter of a bullock* in his mouth," swimming around with his prize, just where the seamen had been bathing the evening before. The "young gentlemen," who had enjoyed the bath, watched with horror the monster, which, at first, was supposed to be a whale, and for whose bloody jaws, armed with its rows of savage teeth, they would have been only dainty morsels. The great bay between St. Catharine's and the Continent held every eye, as the Essex floated gracefully, proudly away from her anchorage. "Handsome villages and houses built around, shores which gradually ascend in mountains, covered to their summit with trees which remain in constant verdure; a climate always temperate and healthy; small islands scattered here and there, equally covered with verdure, the soil extremely productive; all combine to render it, in appearance, the most delightful country in the world." Heavy gales and cooler weather changed the aspect of life in the frigate, which had been one of romantic and pleasant adventure. Three months had passed since she left the Delaware, only seven days of which were spent in port, and close economy in stores became necessary. Again and again the commander alludes to the surprising health of the crew, which his own unwearied care doubtless secured.

The wild albatross with other sea-birds, and in the waters the whale and dolphin, sported around the ship, attracting not only the curiosity of the seamen unaccustomed to the sights, but their weapons of capture. The supplies were getting low, and there was occasion for uneasiness among the men, which was anticipated and prevented by the unceasing and paternal vigilance of the commander. With such officers on all our great ships, we should not have the sad and horrid tales of tyranny and mutiny which disgrace the annals of the marine.

The Essex now directed her course toward Cape Horn, the dread of the mariner who is compelled to turn this tempestuous point. You can imagine, young reader, the lively interest with which David looked away to the savage coast of Terra del Fuego—the "land of fire"—of which we all learn in the early school lessons. The frigate ventured as near as it was safe to do, seeking a haven. The distant hills were seen clothed with verdure, while the less conspicuous features of the country were concealed from observation by the haziness of the weather, to the intense regret of those to whom the voyage was new; "the fog," says the captain, "preventing a clearer view of a coast which has excited so much the attention of mankind, from the description given by the most celebrated navigators."

Unable to gain anchorage in the Bay of Good Success, whose name tells the story of its grateful shelter, and is fully described, first by Captain Cook, the Essex ploughed the rough sea to the bleak Cape San Diego, whose scene of utter desolation spread a gloom over the sensitive, homesick heart. Even the cheerful, fearless Porter declares: "The appearance was dreary beyond description. Perhaps, however, the critical situation of the ship, the foaming of the breakers, the violence of the wind, and the extreme haziness of the weather, may, all combined, have served to render the appearance more dreadful. But from the impression made by its appearance then, and from the description given by others, I am induced to believe that no part of the world presents a more horrible aspect than Staten Island. The breakers appeared to lie about half a mile from the shore; while we were standing off, the whole sea, from the violence of the current, appeared in a foam of breakers, and nothing but the apprehension of immediate destruction could have induced me to venture through it. But, thanks to the excellent qualities of the ship, we received no material injury; although we were pitching our forecastle under with a heavy press of sail, and the violence of the sea was such that it was impossible for any man to stand without grasping something to support himself. Our making the breakers in the manner we did proved most fortunate; for had we passed through the straits without discovering the land (which would have been the case had we been one mile further north), I should have supposed myself to the east of Staten Island; and after running the distance which I believed necessary to clear Cape St. John's, have steered a course that would have entangled us in the night with the rocks and breakers about Cape Horn. Had this happened, thick and hazy as the weather continued, our destruction would have been inevitable, as we could not have seen the danger one hundred yards from the ship, had we even been apprehensive and on the lookout for it, which would not have been the case."

All this was a fresh and inspiring acquaintance with ocean life to Midshipman Farragut; it was "seeing the world," as the home among the Cumberland summits and cruising along our sea-border had never presented it to his brave young spirit, which was at last in its congenial atmosphere of adventure and culture. And I must let you read his captain's description of the encounter with the treacherous, tempestuous Cape, again revealing, unconsciously, his own unselfish regard for his ship's company: "So different was the temperature of the air, the appearance of the heavens, and the smoothness of the sea, to every thing we had expected and pictured to ourselves, that we could not but smile at our own credulity and folly in giving credit to (what we supposed) the exaggerated and miraculous accounts of former voyages; and even when we admitted, for a moment, the correctness of their statements, we could not help attributing their disasters and misfortunes chiefly to their own imprudences and mismanagement. As we had endeavored to guard against every accident that we had to apprehend, we flattered ourselves with the belief that fortune would be more favorable to our enterprise than she had been to theirs. But, while we were indulging ourselves in these pleasing speculations, the black clouds hanging over Cape Horn burst upon us with a fury we little expected, and reduced us in a few minutes to a reefed foresail and close-reefed main-topsail, and in a few hours afterwards to our storm-staysails. Nor was the violence of the winds the only danger we had to encounter; for it produced an irregular and dangerous sea, that threatened to jerk away our masts at every roll of the ship. With this wind we steered to the southward, with a view of getting an offing from the land, in expectation of avoiding, in future, the sudden gusts and the irregular seas which we supposed were owing to violent currents, and confined to the neighborhood of the coast. But in this expectation we were much disappointed, for, as we receded from the coast, the gale increased; and it was in vain that we hoped for that moderate and pleasant weather which former navigators have generally experienced in the latitude of 60° south, which we reached on the 18th. From the time we lost sight of the land until this period, the gales blew hard from the northwest, accompanied with heavy rains, cold disagreeable weather, and a dangerous sea. We were never enabled to carry more sail than a close-reefed main-topsail and reefed foresail, and were frequently under our storm-staysails. But by keeping the ship a point free, she made but little lee-way, went fast through the water, and gave us considerable westing, though we were carrying a heavy press of sail, and were frequently deluged with the sea that broke into us. The movement of every passing cloud was anxiously watched, every appearance of the heavens carefully noted, and our chief employment was comparing the weather we had experienced, and present appearances, with the accounts of those who had preceded us.

"The eclipse of the moon, on the 14th, had prepared us to meet with bad weather; and we felt much gratified to believe it all over, the weather having now become more moderate. As we were as far to the west as Cook on his first voyage, and nearly as far as La Perouse, when they stood to the northward, and as we had run this distance from the straits of Le Maire in as short a time as it had ever been done by any ship, we were willing to believe ourselves the favorite children of fortune; for the weather we had yet met had not been so severe as some we had encountered on the coast of North America during our last cruise, and fell far short of the descriptions given by the author of Lord Anson's voyage. On the afternoon of the 18th a gale came on from the westward, which, for its violence, equalled any described by that historian. We were enabled to force the ship about two knots, through a tremendous head sea, which threatened every moment destruction to our bowsprit and masts. The gale, however, increasing, we were soon reduced to the main storm-staysail, and from that to bare poles. About 12 o'clock the wind hauled around to the southwest, and blew in dreadful squalls, accompanied with hail, and this enabled us to steer northwest. The squalls came at intervals of from fifteen to twenty minutes, with so little warning, and with such tremendous blasts, that it was impossible to shorten sail; for to have started the sheets after they had struck the ship, would have been attended with the certain loss of the sail. I therefore saw no alternative but running before the wind while they lasted, and as soon as they were over, which was generally in two or three minutes, hauled again by the wind. Thus, by the utmost attention and care, we were enabled to get along at the rate of between five and six miles per hour; and on the 21st found ourselves, by estimation, in the latitude of 57° 30′ south, and the longitude of 77° west. And having now no doubt of succeeding speedily in my passage to a friendly port, where we could get supplies, I, to the great joy of all on board, ordered the allowance of bread to be increased to two-thirds.

"The weather had for some days been piercing cold; this, with the almost constant rains and hails, and the water shipped from the heavy seas, and from leaks, kept the vessel very uncomfortable, and the clothes of the officers and crew very uncomfortably wet. The extremities of those who had formerly been affected by the frost became excessively troublesome to them, so much so as to prevent some from doing their duty; from this cause I myself was a considerable sufferer. Many, also, felt severely the great want of shoes, and the necessary quantity of woollen clothing. Their allowance of provisions was barely sufficient to satisfy the cravings of nature; and as to refreshments of any kind, they were entirely out of the question, our scanty supply obtained at St. Catharine's having been long consumed. The fatigues of the officers and crew (although I endeavored to alleviate them as much as possible, by only keeping the watch on deck) were very considerable, for deceitful intervals of moderate weather would for a moment encourage us to make sail, when, in a few minutes afterwards, blasts, accompanied with rain and hail, would threaten destruction to our sails and spars. We had felt apprehensive of a current setting constantly to the eastward, but did not believe that it could in two days have taken us four degrees to the eastward of our reckoning. But great and mortifying as this discovery was to us, it was not to be overcome but by renewed efforts and fortitude; and as the wind came round to the northward, it gave us a prospect of soon recovering our lost ground. I therefore permitted the crew to continue to draw their increased allowance of bread, as I did not wish them to feel the extent of my disappointment; which, perhaps, would have been attended with a depression of their spirits, and might have produced that dreaded disease, the scurvy, from which we have been hitherto exempt in a most extraordinary degree, not the least sympton yet appearing on board. The crew, notwithstanding their constant labor, fatigue, and privations, have enjoyed most extraordinary spirits. They continued their usual diversions during the gales; labored with cheerfulness when labor was requisite; not a murmur or complaint was heard, but all seemed determined to share with their officers every fatigue, and to exert themselves to the utmost to conquer every difficulty. To be sure we had not been long in those seas, but since we had left America they have been deprived of almost every comfort of life; and so great was their desire now for fresh provisions that a rat was esteemed a dainty, and pet monkeys were sacrificed to appease their longings. Our provisions and water still continued good; the bread, to be sure, had been attacked by worms and weevils, but they had only in a slight degree altered its qualities. Our peas and beans, however, had not escaped so well; for, as in this cold climate the allowance of water enabled us to spare enough to permit the boiling and use of them, I directed them to be served; but on opening the barrels that contained them, we found only a mass of chaff and worms. The rats, also, had found the way into our bread-rooms, and had occasioned a great consumption of that precious article. As to our water, none could be sweeter or purer; it had not undergone the slightest change. And the only fact I think it necessary to state in support of this assertion is, that a live mullet, nearly three-quarters of an inch in length, was this day pumped from a cask filled with the water in the river Delaware; had this water undergone any corruption, the fish could not certainly have existed in it. This little fish I have put in a bottle of its native water, with a view of preserving it alive. From its size, I should suppose it to have been produced from the spawn while in the cask. The water taken in at St.

Catharine's was found to be equally good; and my own experience now enables me to assure all navigators, that the only precaution necessary to have good water at sea is, to provide casks made of well-seasoned staves, have them cleansed, and filled with pure water. Should it be necessary at any time (for the trim or safety of the ship, which is sometimes the case) to fill them with salt water, particular care must be taken that they be filled and well soaked and cleansed with fresh water before they are filled with the water intended for use. These particulars, as I have before observed, have never been neglected by me since I had the command of a vessel, and consequently no one on board has ever suffered from the use of bad water. This is an object that well merits the attention of every commander, when the chief comfort and the health of his crew are so much dependent thereon. For who has experienced, at sea, a greater enjoyment than a draught of pure water? Or who can say that the ship-fever and scurvy do not originate frequently in the disgusting water which seamen are too often driven to the necessity of drinking at sea, even when their stomachs revolt at it?

"On the 24th, after experiencing a heavy gale from the northwest, I had the extreme satisfaction to find ourselves as far to the westward as 80°; and as the wind shifted and blew from the southwest, I had no doubt of being able to effect our passage into the Pacific Ocean.

I consequently thought it advisable to increase the allowance of water, in order that the crew might be enabled to spare enough to afford them tea morning and evening, as I was convinced it would conduce as much to their health as their comfort. When I communicated to them this arrangement, I took an opportunity of thanking them for their good conduct during our boisterous and unpleasant passage around the Cape; encouraged them to a continuance of it, by holding out prospects of indulgence to those who should so distinguish themselves; and, as some thefts had been committed, for which the perpetrators were then under the punishment of wearing a yoke, I gave a general pardon on condition that the first offender brought to the gangway should receive three dozen lashes.

"It was with no little joy we now saw ourselves fairly in the Pacific Ocean, and calculated on a speedy end to all our sufferings. We began also to form our projects for annoying the enemy, and had already equipped, in imagination, one of their vessels of fourteen or sixteen guns, and manned from the Essex, to cruise against their commerce; indeed, various were the schemes we formed at this time for injuring them, and we had already, in fancy, immense wealth to return with to our country. As the gale continued to blow from the southwest every hour seemed to brighten our prospects and give us fresh spirits; and on the last of February, being in the latitude of 50° south, the wind became moderate and shifted to the northward, the sea smooth, and every prospect of mild and pleasant weather. I consequently determined to replace the guns and get the spars on the spar-deck; but before we had effected this, the wind had freshened up to a gale, and by noon had reduced us to our storm-staysail and close-reefed main-topsail. It hauled around to the westward in the afternoon, and blew with a fury even exceeding any thing we had yet experienced, bringing with it such a tremendous sea as to threaten us every moment with destruction. Our sails, our standing and running rigging, from the succession of bad weather, had become so damaged, as to be no longer trustworthy; we took, however, the best means in our power to render every thing secure, and carried as heavy a press of sail as the ship would bear, to keep her from drifting on the coast of Patagonia, which we had reason to believe was not far distant, from the appearance of birds, kelp, and whales, which I have heretofore found to be tolerably sure indications of a near approach to land, and from the clouds to leeward, which appeared as if arrested by the high mountains of the Andes. From the excessive violence with which the wind blew, we had strong hopes that it would be of short continuance; until, worn out with fatigue and anxiety, greatly alarmed with the terrors of a lee-shore, and in momentary expectation of the loss of our masts and bowsprit, we almost considered our situation hopeless. To add to our distress, our pumps had become choked by the shingle ballast, which, from the violent rolling of the ship, had got into them; the ship made a great deal of water, and the sea had increased to such a height as to threaten to swallow us at every instant; the whole ocean was one continued foam of breakers, and the heaviest squall that I ever before experienced had not equalled in violence the most moderate intervals of this hurricane. We had done all that lay in our power to preserve the ship from the violence of the elements, and turned our attention to the pumps (which we were enabled to clear), and to keep the ship from drifting on shore, by getting on the most advantageous tack. We, however, were not enabled to wear but once, for the violence of the wind and sea was such as afterwards to render it impossible to attempt it without hazarding the destruction of the ship and the loss of every life on board. The whole of the 1st and 2d of March we anxiously hoped for a change, but in vain; our fatigues had been constant and excessive; many had been severely bruised by being thrown, by the violent jerks of the ship, down the hatchways, and I was particularly unfortunate in receiving three severe falls, which at length disabled me from going on deck. The gale had already blown three days without abating; the ship had resisted its violence to the astonishment of all, without having received any considerable injury; and we began to hope, from her buoyancy and other good qualities, we should be enabled to weather the gale. We had shipped several heavy seas that would have proved destructive to almost any other ship; but to us they were attended with no other inconveniences than the momentary alarm they excited, and that arising from the immense quantity of water which forced its way into every part of the vessel, and kept every thing afloat between decks. However, about three o'clock of the morning of the 3d, the watch only being on deck, an enormous sea broke over the ship, and for an instant destroyed every hope. Our gun-deck ports were burst in; both boats on the quarters stove; our spare spars washed from the chains; our head-rails washed away, hammock-stanchions burst in, and the ship perfectly deluged and water-logged immediately after this tremendous shock. The gale, however, soon after began to abate, and in the morning we were enabled to set our reefed foresail. In the height of the gale, Lewis Price, a marine, who had long been confined with a pulmonary complaint, departed this life, and was this morning committed to the deep; but the violence of the sea was such that the crew could not be permitted to come on deck to attend the ceremony of his burial, as their weight would have strained and endangered the safety of the ship.

"When this last sea broke on board us, one of the prisoners, the boatswain of the Nocton, through excess of alarm exclaimed that the ship's broadside was stove in, and that she was sinking. This alarm was greatly calculated to increase the fears of those below, who, from the immense torrent of water that was rushing down the hatchways, had reason to believe the truth of his assertion. Many who were washed from the spar to the gun-deck, and from their hammocks, and did not know the extent of the injury, were also greatly alarmed; but the men at the wheel, and some others, who were enabled by a strong grasp to keep their stations, distinguished themselves by their coolness and activity after the shock. I took this opportunity of advancing them one grade, by filling up the vacancies occasioned by those sent in prizes and those who were left at St. Catharine's; rebuking, at the same time, the others for their timidity.

"And now we began to hope for better times, for the sky became serene, and we were enabled to make sail; the wind shifted to the S. W., and brought with it the only pleasant weather we had experienced since we passed the Falkland Islands. Here again we were deceived, for before night it began to blow in heavy squalls, with cold rain, and reduced us to close-reefed fore and main topsails, and reefed foresail. But as the wind was fair, we consoled ourselves with the pleasing reflection that we were every moment receding further from the influence of the dreary and inhospitable climate of Cape Horn. On the 5th of the month, having passed the parallel of Chili, our sufferings appeared at an end, for we enjoyed pleasant and temperate weather, with fine breezes from the southward;

and, for the first time during our passage, were enabled to knock out our dead-lights, and open our gun-deck ports. The repairs of our damages went on rapidly, and by night the ship was in every respect, excepting wear and tear, as well prepared for active service as the day we left St. Catharine's. Our latitude at meridian was 39° 20′ south; and we had a distant view of part of the Andes, which appeared covered with snow. Albatrosses were as usual about the ship; several fish, by sailors denominated sun-fish, were seen; and we frequently passed a white and apparently gelatinous substance, which we had not an opportunity of examining. There was every prospect of a speedy arrival in some port on the coast of Chili, and I directed the cables to be bent, using every means in our power to guard them from the effects of rocky bottom.

"The health of the crew was better than when I left the United States, and not the slightest appearance of scurvy in the ship. We were all in high spirits, and in momentary expectation of falling in with some of the enemy's ships. It was my intention now to look into Mocha, a small uninhabited island on the coast of Chili, in the latitude of about 38° 15′, and about eight leagues distant from the coast. This place, I had understood, was a resort for the British vessels employed in smuggling, and in the whale fishery on the coast; and from thence I intended to proceed to St. Maria, another uninhabited island further north, also frequented by them. From those vessels I hoped to be enabled to procure such provisions and other supplies as we were in want of, and thereby render our going into Conception unnecessary, as I was desirous of doing the enemy as much injury as possible, without giving any alarm on the coast."

On the morning of March 6th the seamen saw, twenty miles away, the dark outline of Mocha, rising, like an Egyptian pyramid from its sea of yellow sand, above the blue main. A few hours later the frigate anchored, and the boats were among the breakers. With spy-glasses animals had been discovered, and the men were all excitement to get at them and supply the exhausted larder with fresh meat, without which, that scourge of sea-life, the scurvy, makes sad havoc. The boats find a landing, and "crack! crack!" go the muskets, in the chase after wild hogs, till, at dusk, more than a dozen lie in the small craft, bound for the Essex. And now a tragedy occurred which threw a deep shadow over the crew, and the account of which further exhibits the fine qualities of Capt. Porter's character, the influence of which was very great over all on board, but especially so upon the "young gentlemen," many of whom were taken from indulgent homes. He records of this evening hunt: "Seeing a drove of horses coming along, and every one being anxious to fire, and feeling apprehensive of some accident,

I directed them to conceal themselves behind the boats that were hauled on the beach, and not to fire until I had fired, intending to reserve my shot till they had got a position where all could fire without the least danger of accident. I accordingly fired, and was succeeded by a volley; one horse was crippled, and the seamen ran forward with clubs to knock him down. They already had hold of him, when a young officer, who had the misfortune of being very near-sighted (and who had reserved his fire, not having seen the drove), ran forward, and seeing, in the dark, the group of sailors about the animal, supposed it to be the horses, and fired. Unhappily the ball passed through the breast of James Spafford, the gunner's mate, one of the best and most trusty men in my ship. It is impossible for me to express what were my feelings, when, with the utmost composure, the poor fellow, with a firm voice, said, 'Sir, you have shot me! I am a dying man; take me to the boat.' The distress of the officer on the occasion was beyond description. Dr. Hoffman was on shore, and gave us but little hopes of his life, as the ball had entered his right breast, and came out below his right shoulder, near the backbone. A boat was immediately sent off to the ship with him, accompanied by Dr. Hoffman and the officer who had so unfortunately been the cause of the disaster; and on my arrival, which was speedily after him, I found him still alive, but the chief surgeon, Dr. Miller, could give me no reason to believe that he would recover. Had it not been for this dreadful accident we should have been much delighted with our excursion on shore, as it had not only afforded us a pleasant recreation after our excessive fatigues at sea, but had enabled us to extend the benefits of it to the whole ship's company, as we had been so successful as to procure a fresh mess for all hands. The horse-meat, however, was generally preferred to the hogs, it being much fatter and more tender; the hogs proved tough, and had besides (to me) an unpleasant flavor, though I heard no complaints among the sailors on that subject, as their stomachs were perhaps less delicate.

"It was much to be regretted that I had been so imprudently indulgent as to permit so many to take muskets on shore, on many accounts; but more particularly on account of the accident which happened to poor Spafford. The constant firing, by bad marksmen, in every direction, not only greatly alarmed the horses and hogs, but made them very shy. This prevented the more skilful from having an opportunity of killing them; but many of the poor animals were wounded in different parts of the body, and made their escape with the blood streaming from their wounds; whereas expert marksmen would not have fired until they were sure of shooting them through some vital part."

Cruelty is, indeed, a crime. There is no nobler animal

than the horse, and none is more abused by passionate, domineering man. The voice of God and humanity is, "Blessed are the merciful!" a quality which has always graced the character of DAVID GLASCOE FARRAGUT.

CHAPTER VIII.

Sailing in the Fog—Valparaiso—A glad Sight—The Welcome—Novel Scenes—An expected Battle—Life in Chili—Down the Coast—A strange Hermit—Ocean Scenes—The Sailor's Punishment and Escape—Sail ho!—A brief Order—The Tortoise—A Tomb and Epitaph.

THE cruising ground of the wide Pacific was now before the Essex. A "sharp lookout" was kept by her men for an English sail, which, it was thought, would be likely to pass between Conception and Valparaiso. But a heavy fog curtained the frigate, through which the enemy could not be seen a mile distant, but through it the roar of the dreaded breakers came, whenever the vessel approached the highlands of the coast. "On the latter part of March 12th light airs sprang up from the southwest, the weather began to clear off slowly, and every eye was engaged in searching for a sail, as the fog moved to leeward. Nothing, however, was to be seen but a wide expanse of ocean, bounded on the east by the dreary, barren, and iron-bound coast of Chili, at the back of which the eternally snow-capped mountains of the Andes reared their lofty heads, and altogether presented to us a scene of gloomy solitude, far exceeding any thing I ever before experienced. No vessels of any description, or the least trace of the existence of a human being, was discovered on the coast, except in one instance, when a fire was lighted in the evening in a small cove, probably by some Indians, or persons engaged in smuggling, and intended, no doubt, as an invitation to land."

Rounding a bold point on the 14th, the city of Valparaiso gladdened the sight of the men of the Essex; the long sandy beach; the mountain-path to the town, along which wound a drove of loaded mules; the colors of the harbor-shipping flying; the grim battery guarding it; all burst upon the view from behind a mountain of rocks, spreading a murmur of delight over the decks of the frigate. The cordial welcome from the authorities was unexpected and cheering, the people having shaken off Spanish rule and opened their ports to all nations. They desired American protection, and offered every friendly attention. Soon the thunder of salutes rolled over the harbor, and the crew rejoiced in the prospect of touching land again and replenishing their stores. Mr. Poinsett was then our consul-general in Chili, and messages were immediately sent to him.

Many of the Chilians had never before seen a frigate, and stared at its rows of ordnance, while numbers of the crew, who not till then had looked upon the natives, curiously watched *them*. Then commenced the more pleasing work of pouring into the Essex the cartloads of fruit; apples, peaches, nectarines, melons, and vegetables were heaped up until there was no more room. Pigs and fowls were brought in droves and flocks; when, at length, the captain found they would *crowd his men*, unless he stopped making a Noah's ark of his frigate, and so he limited the number of the former to less than *two hundred*.

All on board were greatly amused by the uses to which the hides of the abundant wild cattle are applied; and you will not wonder when you know that "the most of the furniture for their mules and horses, and their houses, and, on some parts of the coast, even their boats, or (as they are called) balsas, are made of this article. It is used for every purpose to which it is possible to apply it, either whole, cut in pieces, or in long strips. When used for balsas, two hides, each cut something in the form of a canoe, with the seam upward, are blown up by means of a reed, and strapped together; a piece of board is then laid across to sit on, and on this frail machine they venture a considerable distance to sea. The *laque*, for the use of which the Chilians are so famous, is formed of a very long strip of hide, with a running noose; and their dexterity in using it, in catching animals at full speed, is surprising. Every pack-horseman and driver of a jackass is furnished with one of these; and so much do they delight in them, or in showing their dexterity, that when they wish to catch any one of their drove, either to load or unload, or for any other purpose, they take their distance, deliberately coil up their *laque*, and never fail of throwing it over the neck of the animal wanted."

Brilliant parties were given by the people for the benefit of the Essex; and in regard to the ladies, the Yankee guests thought notwithstanding the paint their "features were agreeable, and their large dark eyes remarkably brilliant and expressive. Were it not for their bad teeth, occasioned by the too liberal use of the matti, they would, notwithstanding the Chilian tinge, be thought handsome, particularly by those who had been so long as we out of the way of seeing any women."

The matti is a decoction of the herb of Paraguay, sweetened with sugar, and sucked hot through a long silver tube. To the use of this beverage the Chilians are perfect slaves. The taste is pleasant, but it makes terrible havoc with the teeth. *Tobacco slaves* cannot reproach the South Americans for their devotion to the matti; and we cannot refrain here from expressing the hope that the youthful reader sails clear of both *rum-reefs*, and the dirty shoals of the vile weed, where health and morals are often impaired, if not ruined.

Suddenly the appearance of a sail interrupted social

enjoyments, and the crew hastened to their stations, and the Chilians to the hill-sides, in expectation of a naval engagement. But the Portuguese colors quickly disappointed both parties, when an "invitation was brought to the frigate to dine and spend the evening with the governor, who, it was seen by the flags about the battery in front of his house, had made great preparations for the occasion; the entertainment was given by the order and at the expense of the superior government of Chili. The company were seated in an extensive tent, handsomely and fancifully decorated with the flags of different nations, and the ground covered with rich carpets; the dinner was served up in silver plate, and, with the exception of the blades of the knives alone, no other metal or substance whatever was used for any part of the table equipage. The dinner consisted of at least twenty changes; and by the time the third course had been removed, the guests had cause to regret that they had not reserved their appetites for some of the delicacies which we perceived were likely to succeed the substantial food of the first course, with which the keen appetites were soon cloyed. The officers of the Portuguese ship, and some English merchants, were also at table; but when the wine began to circulate, and the Chilian officers to feel the ardor of their patriotism, such flaming toasts were given as to make them think it prudent to retire."

These retiring officers evidently *did not relish* the compliments the wine gained for the United States. The next day the Essex weighed anchor for the "high seas."

With the last week in March came the renewed chase after prizes off the coast of Callao, where poor Spafford, who was wounded in the horse-hunt, died, and was buried in the deep according to the Episcopal service, which, always impressive, is never more so than on the ocean.

Two curious phenomena were witnessed here—the sea filled with craw-fish, tinging the water blood-red, and in other places covered with pelicans and various aquatic birds, beneath whose shadow ran schools of fish, which, says the commander, "were to be seen in great numbers, constantly pursued by seals, bonetas, and porpoises; and such as attempted to escape their ravenous jaws by jumping out of the water, were immediately snapped up by the innumerable swarms of birds that were hovering over them.

"On our arrival off Ajugia, we had another opportunity of witnessing a similar scene; and as the water was perfectly smooth and the winds light, we were enabled to examine it more minutely. We discovered the sea boiling violently in many places; and wherever this was the case, vast numbers of seals, large fish, and birds, were apparently in pursuit of small fish. On approaching one of these places, the water had so much the appearance of having been put into action by violent currents, opposed by sunken rocks, that I felt some uneasiness, and directed the helm to be put a-weather to avoid it; however, the next one had the same appearance, and was equally attended by fish. I therefore steered close to it, and saw that in the centre of the agitated spot (which bore the appearance of water boiling in a pot) were myriads of small fish, collected together, and appeared as though it were impossible for them to escape from this violent whirlpool, which was so powerful as to affect considerably the steerage of the ship. Whether this boiling of the water was occasioned by the vast numbers of seals and large fish which kept constantly darting in among the small fry, which were drawn as it were to a focus, I will not pretend to say. It is possible, however, that whales, or some fish perhaps nearly as large as whales, which did not show themselves above the surface, might also have been concerned in the pursuit, and occasioned the agitation that so much surprised us; for I cannot think it possible that the seals and bonetas, numerous as they were, could have produced so violent a commotion."

The Essex sails over the comparatively tranquil waters of the *Pacific* toward the Gallipagos Islands, in search of English whalers, giving the "young gentlemen" an acquaintance with that *largest kind of fishing.* To many of them, the first view of a ship for this perilous business, with its boats for harpooning, its try-kettles for separating the oil from blubber, the tackle which holds the monster, sometimes nearly a hundred feet in length, to the side of the vessel till stripped of the coating of fat, was a new spectacle. And to think of those vessels for three or four years in distant seas, till the value of the oil has reached often more than $100,000, when the crews return home to find both pleasant and mournful changes in their dwellings, and the communities around them!

I must give you here a letter found in the harbor of Charles' Island, by Lieutenant Downes, over which the people of the Essex had a laugh:

June 14th, 1812.

Ship Sukey, John Macy 7½ Months out 150 Barrels 75 days from Lima No oil Since Leaving that Port. Spanyards Very Savage Lost on the Braziel Bank John Sealin Apprentice to Capt Benjamin Worth Fell from the fore top sail Yard In A Gale of Wind. Left Diana Capt paddock 14 day Since 250 Barrels I Leave this port this Day With 250 Turpen 8 Boat Load Wood Yesterday Went Up to Patts Landing East Side. to the Starboard hand of the Landing 1½ Miles Saw 100 Turpen 20 Rods A part Road Very Bad

Yours Forevir

John Macy.

There is a strange, and though in low life, a romantic story alluded to in this epistle which does not speak well for the early education of Captain Macy, affording you another glimpse of the unwritten history of many a stray representative of our common humanity, in the solitudes of land and sea.

"Lieutenant Downes saw on the rocks with which the bay was in many parts skirted, several seals and pelicans, some of which he killed; but, on searching diligently the shore, was unable to find any land tortoises, though they no doubt abound in other parts of the island. Doves were seen in great numbers, and were so easily approached that several of them were knocked over with stones. While our boat was on shore, Captain Randall sent his boat to a small beach in the same bay, about a mile from where our boat landed, and in a short time she returned loaded with fine green turtle, two of which he sent us, and we found them excellent. It may be seen by Captain Macy's letter, that on the east side of the island there is another landing, which he calls Pat's landing; and this place will probably immortalize an Irishman named Patrick Watkins, who some years since left an English ship and took up his abode on this island, and built himself a miserable hut, about a mile from the landing called after him, in a valley containing about two acres of ground capable of cultivation, and perhaps the only spot on the island which affords sufficient moisture for the purpose. Here he succeeded in raising potatoes and pumpkins in considerable quantities, which he generally exchanged for rum, or sold for cash. The appearance of this man, from the accounts I have received of him, was the most dreadful that can be imagined; ragged clothes, scarce sufficient to cover his nakedness, and covered with vermin; his red hair and beard matted, his skin much burnt from constant exposure to the sun, and so wild and savage in his manner and appearance that he struck every one with horror. For several years this wretched being lived by himself on this desolate spot, without any apparent desire than that of procuring rum in sufficient quantities to keep himself intoxicated, and, at such times, after an absence from his hut of several days, he would be found in a state of perfect insensibility, rolling among the rocks of the mountains. He appeared to be reduced to the lowest grade of which human nature is capable, and seemed to have no desire beyond the tortoises and other animals of the island, except that of getting drunk. But this man, wretched and miserable as he may have appeared, was neither destitute of ambition nor incapable of undertaking an enterprise that would have appalled the heart of any other man; nor was he devoid of the talent of rousing others to second his hardihood.

"He by some means became possessed of an old musket, and a few charges of powder and ball; and the possession of this weapon, probably first stimulated his ambition. He felt himself strong as the sovereign of the island, and was desirous of proving his strength on the first human being that fell in his way, which happened to be a negro, who was left in charge of a boat belonging to an American ship that had touched there for refreshments. Patrick came down to the beach where the boat lay, armed with his musket, now become his constant companion, directed the negro, in an authoritative manner, to follow him, and on his refusal snapped his musket at him twice, which luckily missed fire. The negro, however, became intimidated, and followed him. Patrick now shouldered his musket, marched off before, and on his way up the mountains exultingly informed the negro that he was henceforth to work for him, and become his slave, and that his good or bad treatment would depend on his future conduct. On arriving at a narrow defile, and perceiving Patrick off his guard, the negro seized the moment, grasped him in his arms, threw him down, tied his hands behind, shouldered him, and carried him to his boat, and when the crew had arrived he was taken on board the ship. An English smuggler was lying in the harbor at the same time, the captain of which sentenced Patrick to be severely whipped on board both vessels, which was put in execution, and he was afterwards taken on shore handcuffed by the Englishmen, who compelled him to make known where he had concealed the few dollars he had been enabled to accumulate from the sale of his potatoes and pumpkins, which they took from him. But while they were busy in destroying his hut and garden the wretched being made his escape, and concealed himself among the rocks in the interior of the island until the ship had sailed, when he ventured from his hiding-place, and by means of an old file, which he drove into a tree, freed himself from the handcuffs. He now meditated a severe revenge, but concealed his intentions. Vessels continued to touch there, and Patrick, as usual, to furnish them with vegetables; but from time to time he was enabled, by administering potent draughts of his darling liquor to some of the men of their crews, and getting them so drunk that they were rendered insensible, to conceal them until the ship had sailed; when, finding themselves entirely dependent on him, they willingly enlisted under his banners, became his slaves, and he the most absolute of tyrants. By this means he had augmented the number to five, including himself, and every means was used by him to endeavor to procure arms for them, but without effect. It is supposed that his object was to have surprised some vessel, massacre her crew, and take her off. While Patrick was meditating his plans, two ships, an American and an English vessel, touched there, and applied to Patrick for vegetables. He promised them the greatest abundance, provided they would send their boats to his landing, and their people to bring them from his garden, informing them that his rascals had become so indolent of late that he could not get them to work. This arrangement was agreed to; two boats were sent from each vessel and hauled on the beach. Their crews all went to Patrick's habitation, but neither he nor any of his people were to be found; and, after waiting until their patience was exhausted, they returned to the beach, where they found only the wreck of three of their boats, which were broken to pieces, and the fourth one missing. They succeeded, however, after much difficulty, in getting around to the bay opposite to their ships, where other boats were sent to their relief; and the commanders of the ships, apprehensive of some other trick, saw no security except in a flight from the island, leaving Patrick and his gang in quiet possession of the boat. But before they sailed they put a letter in a keg, giving intelligence of the affair, and moored it in the bay, where it was found by Captain Randall, but not until he had sent his boat to Patrick's landing for the purpose of procuring refreshments; and, as may be easily supposed, he felt no little inquietude until her return, when she brought him a letter from Patrick to the following purport, which was found in his hut:

"'SIR: I have made repeated applications to captains of vessels to sell me a boat, or to take me from this place, but in every instance met with a refusal. An opportunity presented itself to possess myself of one, and I took advantage of it. I have been a long time endeavoring, by hard labor and suffering, to accumulate wherewith to make myself comfortable; but at different times have been robbed and maltreated, and in a late instance by Captain Paddock, whose conduct in punishing me, and robbing me of about five hundred dollars in cash and other articles, neither agrees with the principles he professes, nor is it such as his sleek coat would lead one to expect.*

"'On the 29th of May, 1809, I sailed from the enchanted island in the Black Prince, bound to the Marquesas.

"'Do not kill the old hen; she is now sitting, and will soon have chickens.

"'(Signed) FATHERLESS OBERLUS.'

"Patrick arrived alone at Guyaquil in his open boat, the rest who sailed with him having perished for want of water, or, as is generally supposed, were put to death by him on his finding the water to grow scarce. From thence he proceeded to Payta, where he wound himself into the affection of a tawny damsel, and prevailed on her to consent to accompany him back to his enchanted island, the beauties of which he no doubt painted in glowing colors; but, from his savage appearance, he was there considered by the police as a suspicious person, and being found under the keel of a small vessel then ready to be launched, and suspected of some improper inten-

* Captain Paddock was of the Society of Friends.

tions, he was confined in Payta gaol, where he now remains; and probably owing to this circumstance Charles' Island, as well as the rest of the Gallipagos, may remain unpopulated for many ages to come. This reflection may naturally lead us to a consideration of the question concerning the population of the other islands scattered about the Pacific Ocean, respecting which so many conjectures have been hazarded. I shall only hazard one, which is briefly this: that former ages may have produced men equally as bold and as daring as Pat, and women as willing as his fair one to accompany them in their adventurous voyages. And when we consider the issue which might be produced from a union between a red-haired wild Irishman and a copper-colored mixed-blooded squaw, we need not be any longer surprised at the different varieties in human nature.

"If Patrick should be liberated from durance, and arrive with his love at this enchanting spot, perhaps (when neither he nor the Gallipagos are any longer remembered) some future navigator may surprise the world by a discovery of them, and his accounts of the strange people with which they may probably be inhabited. From the source from which they shall have sprung, it does not seem unlikely that they will have one trait in their character which is common to the natives of all the islands in the Pacific, a disposition to appropriate to themselves the property of others. From this circumstance, future speculators may confound their origin with that of all the rest."

About and on these islands, besides guanas, huge tortoises, and seals, were also enormous sharks, which frightened the crew by swimming around the boats in which the men were now rowing, snapping at the oars and threatening to tear the thin plank from the timbers, and leave the inmates of the frail bark in the water, where the ferocious attendants would enjoy the banquet thus unceremoniously spread.

April 23d the Essex was a novel spectacle. She had turned the point of Narborough, expecting to come in sight of prizes; and, so great was the anxiety for the excitement and the *results* of a chase, or even a fight, that the officers and men, down to the boys, hung in every part of the rigging like gigantic spiders in a great white web, watching for a speck of canvas. Suddenly the cry of "Sail, ho!" and then another, made the Essex a hive of busy workers in the preparation for a hunt or battle. But how illusory are human anticipations! Not fleecy clouds, but snowy appearances of the shore in the distance, had deceived them, and onward, as if sullenly watching for *realities*, the frigate ploughed her way through the undulating deep. A landing was made. Here is what the captain says of Narborough and its sailor-hermit: "The whole island is a light and thirsty soil, composed entirely of volcanic matter, and probably owes its origin to no distant period, for the volcanic cinders and other appearances lying on every part of the surface, as well as the innumerable craters and hills composed of ashes and lava, all apparently fresh, and in most parts destitute of verdure, sufficiently prove that they have not long been thrown from the bowels of the ocean. These thirsty mountains, like a sponge, soak from the passing clouds the moisture, which serves to keep alive the scanty vegetation scattered over their sides, but they permit none of it to escape in springs or streams of water for the support of animal life. On the side of a rock at this watering-place we found the names of several English and American ships cut, whose crews had been there; and but a short distance from thence was erected a hut, built of loose stones, but destitute of a roof. In the neighborhood of it were scattered in considerable quantities the bones and shells of land and sea tortoises. This I afterwards understood was the work of a wretched English sailor who had been landed there by his captain, destitute of every thing, for having used some insulting language to him. Here he existed near a year on land tortoises and guanas, and his sole dependence for water was on the precarious supply he could get from the drippings of the rocks; at length, finding that no one was likely to come to take him from thence, and fearful of perishing for the want of water, he formed a determination to attempt at all hazards getting into Banks' Bay, where the ships cruise for whales. With this view he provided himself with two seal skins, with which, blown up, he formed a float; and, after hazarding destruction from the sharks, which frequently attacked his vessel, and which he kept off with the stick that served him as a paddle, he succeeded at length in getting alongside an American ship early in the morning, where his unexpected arrival not only surprised but alarmed the crew. His appearance was scarcely human, clothed in the skins of seals, his countenance haggard, thin, and emaciated, his beard and hair long and matted, they supposed him a being from another world. The commander of the vessel where he arrived felt a great sympathy for his sufferings, and determined for the moment to bring to punishment the villain who had, by thus cruelly exposing the life of a fellow-being, violated every principle of humanity." Great amusement was here afforded the men in taking the variety of fine fish, among which was an "enormous sea-lion" secured—sport, the record of which will make the fingers of some of my readers *tingle*.

April 28th, 1813, just as the east glowed with the promise of a beautiful day, to the cot of the heroic commander, where he had "passed a sleepless and anxious night," came the welcome cry again: "Sail, ho! Sail, ho!" which was reëchoed through the Essex with a will. Then she is in harness for the chase, and hour after hour pursues the British whaler, which at nine o'clock is overtaken and soon captured. Before sundown two more graced the *train* of the frigate, boarded and taken by men in open boats, and altogether worth $500,000. And here we have, in the commander's words, a fine improvement of late experiences, valuable to all young people:

"The ease with which the last vessels were taken by our open boats gave us but a poor opinion of British valor; and the satisfaction which the possession of these valuable vessels gave us, made us forget for a moment the hardships of Cape Horn, and the time we had spent without seeing an enemy. It also afforded us a useful lesson, as it convinced us we ought not to despair of success under any circumstances, however unfortunate they may appear; and that, although the patient and persevering may for a time meet with disappointments, Providence will at length give the reward. Slight murmurings had on one or two occasions been heard from some of the crew, occasioned by our want of success heretofore; and with a view of preventing it in future, I considered it advisable to inculcate this maxim by the following note:

"'*April* 30, 1813.

"'SAILORS AND MARINES: Fortune has at length smiled on us, because we deserved her smiles, and the first time she enabled us to display *free trade and sailors' rights*, assisted by your good conduct, she put in our possession near half a million of the enemy's property.

"'Continue to be zealous, enterprising, and patient, and we will yet render the name of the Essex as terrible to the enemy as that of any other vessel, before we return to the United States. My plans shall be made known to you at a suitable period.

"'(Signed) D. PORTER.'"

He also describes the "elephant tortoise," peculiar to this latitude, weighing sometimes three hundred pounds. He walks a foot from the ground, with a heavy motion like the animal after which he is named. "The neck of the tortoise is from eighteen inches to two feet in length, and very slender; their head is proportioned to it, and strongly resembles that of a serpent. But, hideous and disgusting as is their appearance, no animal can possibly afford a more wholesome, luscious, and delicate food than they do; the finest green turtle is no more to be compared to them in point of excellence, than the coarest beef is to the finest veal; and after once tasting the Gallipagos tortoises, every other animal food fell greatly in our estimation. These animals are so fat as to require neither butter nor lard to cook them, and this fat does not possess that cloying quality common to that of most other animals. When tried out, it furnishes an oil superior in taste to that of the olive. The meat of this animal is the easiest of digestion; and a quantity of it, exceeding that of any other food, can be eaten without experiencing the slightest inconvenience. But what seems the most extraordinary in this animal, is the length of time that it can exist without food; for I have been well assured that they have been piled away among the casks in the hold of a ship, where they have been kept eighteen months, and when killed at the expiration of that time, were found to have suffered no diminution in fatness or excellence. They carry with them a constant supply of water, in a bag at the root of the neck, which contains about two gallons, and on tasting that found in those we killed on board, it proved perfectly fresh and sweet. They are very restless when exposed to the light and heat of the sun, but will lie in the dark from one year's end to the other without moving. In the daytime they appear remarkably quick-sighted and timid, drawing their head into their shell on the slightest motion of any object, but they are entirely destitute of hearing, as the loudest noise, even the firing of a gun, does not seem to alarm them in the slightest degree, and at night, or in the dark, they appear perfectly blind. After our tasting the flesh of those animals we regretted that numbers of them had been thrown overboard by the crews of the vessels before their capture, to clear them for action. A few days afterwards, at daylight in the morning, we were so fortunate as to find ourselves surrounded by about fifty of them, which were picked up and brought on board."

Water became the great want, and the islands were

searched for a spring, or the cavity of a rock filled with God's provision for thirst, more desired and refreshing than all the wine of Chili. The fatiguing exploration was rewarded with a partial supply, brought over sharp stones and through hedges of thorns. How the loss of blessings so common enhances their value!

The prizes were painted up, and the little fleet got ready for proceeding on her cruise. The Essex changed her color nearly as readily as the Chameleon, to avoid recognition by any who saw her in a particular dress. One of the last sights on Charles' Island was a solitary *tomb*. Five years before a seaman had been buried there, and at the grave's head a white board with a neatly-engraved epitaph, which, adds Captain Porter, "I give more on account of the extreme simplicity of the verse, and its powerful and flattering appeal to the feelings, than for its elegance or the correctness of the composition:

"'Gentle reader, as you pass by
As you are now, so wonce was I;
As now my body is in the dust,
I hope in heaven my soul to rest.'

"The spot where his remains were deposited was shaded by two lofty thorn-bushes, which afforded an agreeable shade and fragrance, and became the favorite resort of our men at their meals." How lonely is such a resting-place, yet under the ever watchful eye of Him who neither slumbers nor sleeps!

CHAPTER IX.

A new Prize—The Englishmen Scold—List of the Captured Vessels—Volcanic Exhibition—Enchanted Island—Dead Man's Island—A Sad Burial—The "Young Gentlemen" Promoted—Essex Junior—Prizes—James' Island—A Duel—Off for the Washington Islands—Achievements in the Pacific.

ON the 29th of May "Sail, ho!" was heard again; directly ahead was a stranger, immediately pursued by the Essex. Darkness ended the chase till morning, when it was renewed, and the armed vessel surrendered upon demand by Captain Porter. She proved to be the British letter-of-marque ship Atlantic, mounting six guns, a fast-sailing vessel, which made afterwards quite a figure in the growing prize fleet. Scarcely had she been secured before another similar ship was discovered, which, upon being approached, refused to surrender, till a shot flew through the darkness, between the masts. This was the Greenwich, an American, sailing under English colors. When Captain Porter inquired how he could sail under the British flag while his country was engaged in war, he betrayed the same craven spirit we have had to meet in the late rebellion; saying, "He found no difficulty in reconciling it to himself, for, although he was born in America, he was *an Englishman at heart.*" The captive captains flew into a passion, cursing the Government of the United States, and their ill-luck.

These prizes were especially precious on account of their supply of water and various stores, which came in the time of greatest need. The men of the Essex bravely volunteered to go on board the captured ships, even to the midshipmen, until the fleet was manned, and sailed as follows:

The Essex,	mounting	46	guns,	and	245	men,
" Georgiana,	"	16	"	"	42	"
" Atlantic,	"	6	"	"	12	"
" Greenwich,	"	10	"	"	14	"
" Montezuma,	"	2	"	"	10	"
" Policy,		—			10	"
Making in all,		80	guns,		333	men.

The prisoners swelled the number to 420 men.

It is a great compliment to the Essex, that among these desolate islands, while English sailors were continually deserting from the tyranny of their vessels, not one attempted to leave the humane commander of the frigate.

In the afternoon of June 6th, records Captain Porter, "We saw a thick column of smoke rising rapidly as from its centre, ascending to a great height in the air, where it spread off in large white curls, and presented us a grand and majestic spectacle. We soon discovered that one of the numerous volcanoes had burst forth, but there were numerous opinions as to its situation. Some supposed it to be on Narborough, others to the east of Narborough, and on the Island of Albemarle. I was of the latter opinion, which was confirmed next day when we had changed our position. At night the whole atmosphere was illuminated by it, and yet we could perceive neither flames nor sparks thrown out by the crater. The winds now began to freshen from the southeast, and gave us at length some hope of getting from those islands, where we had been so long and unexpectedly delayed by calms and currents. The Spaniards call them the Enchanted Islands, probably from the great difficulty vessels have found in getting from among them. The title seems well applied, and is such a one as I should have felt disposed to give them, had they been destitute of a name. We have been since the 18th of April among them, and the greatest part of the time making every effort in our power to escape."

On the 19th the Essex was off St. Close, or Dead Man's Island, which you will find on the map in the Bay of Guyaquil, receiving its name from its resemblance to a corpse, the head lying toward the west, and is as desolate as a tomb. Here the "best seaman on the ship," John Rodgers, while "somewhat *inebriated*," fell from the mainyard headforemost upon the deck, and shattered his skull, killing him instantly—another victim of rum, which has laid in the dust of shame and death many of the noblest men of all lands. On Dead Man's Island the crew buried poor Rodgers, the prince of the frigate's gunners, with a simple epitaph on the head-board expressing the kindly respect of his comrades:

Entombed here
The body of JOHN RODGERS, seaman, who departed this life
June 19th, 1813, aged 32 years.

Without a sigh
He bid this world adieu;
Without one pang
His fleeting spirit flew.

Look away to that village of reed-houses, called Tumbez, for a view entirely new, certainly to David, and a contrast not unfrequently presented in pagan and tropical countries. The rich soil is covered with cocoa, melons, oranges, sugar-cane, and sweet potatoes, and the verdure glows with perpetual summer. But you see that the frail habitations are elevated by posts some distance above the ground, to keep out the monstrous *alligators* creeping around them.

We come now to a new and important step in the line of promotion to posts of responsibility, for Farragut. The losses by death, and the number of prizes, made additional officers necessary. Captain Porter, therefore, selected from the younger class of the "middies" the reliable boys, to be the nominally prize masters, with able seamen around them. Our hero, then twelve years of age, might have been called the "little captain." Meanwhile, the decks of the Essex rang with cheers, as Lieutenant Downes, who had been away upon a cruise of his own, returned with three prize vessels, some of which were taken after a brisk cannonading, reddening them with the blood of the killed and wounded. These captures increased the fleet to *nine* ships, and a new order of things was inaugurated. The Atlantic, of which you already know something, and will yet learn much more, because the best vessel excepting the Essex, was named the Essex Junior, with a crew of sixty men, and Midshipman Dashiel placed in command. She was to be henceforth also a cruiser. July Fourth! the glorious anniversary—the 36th—dawned upon land and sea, both marked by our struggle with England *to be free!* And hark! how the thunders of ordnance roll out from the little fleet; the smoke curtains it, and almost hides the Stars and Stripes fluttering in the breeze of the torrid zone, while under their glory, shouts arise from all but the *prisoners of war.*

July 12th the Essex pursued and took the piratical Seringapatam, a success which gave peculiar rejoicing to the Yankee captors. The ship was built in India for Tippoo Saib, and was easily made a formidable fighter, mounting twenty-two guns.

The fleet anchored August 5th in the bay between James Island and Albemarle. A curious and amusing scene soon follows: The seamen dot the rigging and line the sides of the vessels, trimming and painting; while others are continually going and coming with boats, engaged in the tortoise hunt. See that boat with thirty large serpent-like heads lifted from its bottom approach the ship's side, and then the awkward prisoners tumbled on board without ceremony, till *fourteen tons* are safely stowed away. No water or food is needed by them for *a year.*

The commander, and Chaplain Adams, rambled over Charles' Island beneath the verdant mangroves, observing the interesting objects described by Captain Calmet, who made the first map of the island. He says:

"At every place where we landed on the western side, we might have walked for miles through long grass, and beneath groves of trees. It only wanted a stream to compose a very charming landscape. This isle appears to have been a favorite resort of the buccaneers, as we not only found seats which had been made by them of earth and stone, but a considerable number of broken jars scattered about, and some entirely whole, in which the Peruvian wine and liquors of that country are preserved. We also found some old daggers, nails, and other implements. This place is, in every respect, calculated for refreshment or relief for crews, after a long and tedious voyage, as it abounds with wood and good anchorage for any number of ships, and sheltered from all winds by Albemarle Isle. The watering-place of the buccaneers was entirely dried up, and there was only found a small rivulet between two hills, running into the sea; the northernmost hill forms the south point of Fresh-water Bay."

A duel at sea! how strangely sound the words. I will let the humane and sorrowful officer of the Essex tell the brief and mournful story: "I have now the painful task of mentioning an occurrence which gave me the utmost pain, as it was attended by the premature death of a promising young officer, whereby the service at this time has received an irreparable injury, and by a practice which disgraces human nature. I shall, however, throw a veil over the whole previous proceedings, and merely state that without my knowledge the parties met on shore at daylight, and at the third fire Mr. Cowan fell dead. His remains were buried the same day in the spot where he fell, and the following inscription was placed over his tomb:

Sacred to the memory
OF LIEUT. JOHN S. COWAN,
Of the U. S. Frigate Essex,
Who died here anno 1813,
Aged 21 years.

His loss is ever to be regretted
By his country;
And mourned by his friends
And brother officers.

"Having entirely changed the appearance of the ship, so that she could not be known from description, or taken for a frigate at a short distance; having made all the repairs which our sails, rigging, boats, etc., required, I buried a letter for Lieutenant Downes, in a bottle at the head of Mr. Cowan's grave, and a duplicate of the same at the foot of a finger-post, erected by me, for the purpose of pointing out to such as may hereafter visit the island the grave of Mr. Cowan."

This tragedy was followed by another that threw the people of the Essex into a state of considerable excitement. Rynard, a quartermaster, and a selfish, ambitious officer, who was always at the head of complaining companies of the seamen when any were to be found, was evidently inclined to get up a mutiny. He was put in irons, then sent to the Seringapatam to be set ashore. The removal of this turbulent spirit restored quiet and order, both enforcing the truth that "one sinner destroyeth much good," and also forming a perfect contrast in character and career, with the Catalonian boy.

Captain Porter thus sums up the achievements to this date, the very last days of August, 1813, of the Essex: "And now I shall notice the important services rendered by our coming into the Pacific. In the first place, by our captures we had completely broken up that important branch of British navigation, the whale-fishery of the coast of Chili and Peru, having captured all their vessels engaged in that pursuit except the ship Comet. By these captures we had deprived the enemy of property to the amount of two and a half millions of dollars, and of the services of three hundred and sixty seamen that I liberated on parole, not to serve against the United States until regularly exchanged. We had effectually prevented them from doing any injury to our own whale-ships, only two of which have been captured, and their captures took place before our arrival. Shortly after my appearance in those seas, our whale-ships, which had taken refuge at Conception and Valparaiso, boldly ventured to sea in pursuit of whales. On the arrival of the Essex Junior at Valparaiso, four of them had returned there with full cargoes, and were waiting for a convoy to protect them some distance from the coast, that they might be enabled to take advantage of the winter season for getting into a port of the United States. This protection Lieutenant Downes was enabled to afford them on his departure thence; and the four ships lying there, as well as my prize, the Policy, sailed in company with him until he had seen them a sufficient distance beyond the usual cruising ground of British armed ships."

What a strange, exciting life for a boy! The changing scenes of the vast ocean, the lookout for an enemy, the chase, the battle often, the gloomily wild and then the enchanting coasts and islands of the tropics, all rendered the experience remarkable, and one rarely enjoyed at any age. I hear young voices exclaim, "I should like to have such a voyage."

There is another side to the mariner's life; exposure, deprivation, and perils. Home, mother, sister, social and Sabbath associations, are not there. But more than this: to be where you can the best *act your part* on

"Life's great field of battle,"

serving God and your country, is the noblest wish and aim of a human heart.

CHAPTER X.

The Cruise to Washington Islands—Cheerfulness—A New Order—A Strange People—Tattooing Incidents—Madison's Island—A Wild Englishman—War among the Islanders—The "Yankees" in the Fray—The Battle and Victory.

HAVING determined to abandon the neighborhood of the Gallipagoes, Captain Porter desired to sail westward along the equator, and find a group of islands comparatively unknown, and thus add discoveries to his conquests. The conscientious *regard to duty*—a quality conspicuous in all distinguished men who have won an honored name—is apparent in the following passage, referring to the attractive hunt for the hidden isles: "But, on reflection, I determined to make the best of my way for the Washington Islands, as this pursuit would have cost some expense of time, an expense I had no right to enter into, as the object of Government in sending me to sea was to annoy the enemy and not to make discoveries; and should any accident happen to the ship in consequence of taking that route, I knew not how

I should be able to justify my conduct in wandering from the direct course to the place of our destination."

The Washington Islands were the next goal of the Essex, but as yet the crew knew nothing of their future cruising ground. I cannot deny my young reader a fresh view of the commander's knowledge of men, and of his official relations in connection with his breaking the secret. "I saw no prospect of evil resulting from making my plans known; and as I have ever considered that cheerfulness is a more powerful antiseptic than any other known, I determined to apply one of the doses which, I believe, had heretofore greatly contributed to preserve the health of my men. The following note was communicated to them; and those who know the disposition of sailors may readily conceive the effect it produced. For the remainder of our passage they could talk and think of nothing but the amusements and novelties that awaited them in this new world:

"'We are bound to the Western Islands, with two objects in view: 1st. That we may put the ship in a suitable condition to enable us to take advantage of the most favorable season for our return home. 2d. I am desirous that you should have some relaxation and amusement after being so long at sea, as from your late good conduct you deserve it.

"'We are going among a people much addicted to thieving, treacherous in their proceedings, whose conduct is governed only by fear, and regulated by views to their interest. We must put nothing in their power, be ever on our guard, and prevent, by every means that can be used, disputes and difficulties with them; we must treat them with kindness, but never trust them, and be most vigilant where there is the greatest appearance of friendship. Let the fate of the many who have been cut off by the savages of the South Sea Islands be a useful warning to us.

"'It will require much discretion and good management to keep up a friendly intercourse with them; and in the regulations that I shall lay down for this object, I shall expect the hearty concurrence of every person under my command.

"'Disputes are most likely to arise from traffic with them. To prevent them I shall appoint a vessel for the express purpose of trading, and shall select an officer and four men to conduct all exchanges. Every other person is positively forbidden to traffic with the natives, except through the persons so selected to conduct the trade.

"'No canoes or male natives will be permitted to come alongside the Essex or any other vessel, except the trading ship, on any account, unless it may be the chief whom I may designate. And if every person exerts himself to carry on the work of the ship, as well as to enforce the above regulations, and such others as I may from time to time adopt, I shall give you time to amuse yourselves on shore. But this indulgence shall cease the moment I discover any relaxation in vigilance or industry. D. PORTER.' "

"Land, ho! Land, ho!" rang from the masthead of the Essex at noon of October 23d, as Hood's Island rose from the sea. The next day the Washington Isles lay in the distance on the bosom of the bright and tranquil deep. Captain Roberts, of Boston, discovered them in May, 1792, and named them after our great General and first President, the *Washington Group*, including Adams, Jefferson, and Hamilton; and presenting, upon getting near them, a beautiful appearance. Rich valleys, clear streams, and houses grouped on the hill-sides, made inviting landscapes to the ocean-weary people of the Essex. The inhabitants, as in the other islands visited, valued very highly pieces of iron and whale's teeth, offering animals and fruits for a small fragment of a hoop, or a single tooth. Sometimes a shipload of sandal wood could be taken from an island for a few of these dental forms of ivory. The natives wore no clothing, and danced, and shouted, and clapped their hands, at the sight of the *old iron hoops*. To my young reader it seems impossible that men could be so like children; but pagans are every way in their infancy, excepting in the comparative innocence of childhood—their passions, as we shall soon see, are full grown in malignity and violence.

For diversion *two* fish-hooks were offered to *three* men for a bread-fruit each held in his hand. To this proposition they agreed. The question was, what would they do with the two hooks? When they had received them, one of the trio sprang into the water with his bread-fruit and swam ashore, settling by his cunning trick of dishonesty the difficulty at once. The "middies" amused themselves with the peculiarities of these primitive specimens of humanity, who seemed to look with awe upon the frigate. Nothing was more curious than the *tattooing* which covered their bodies, often with highly-wrought figures, making the skin like carved mahogany.

The original method among the islanders was the following: "Tattooing is performed by means of a machine made of bone, something like a comb, with the teeth only on one side. The points of the teeth are rubbed with a black paint made of burnt cocoa-nut shell ground to powder, and mixed with water. This is struck into the flesh by means of a heavy piece of wood, which serves the purpose of a hammer. The operation is extremely painful, and streams of blood follow every blow; yet pride induces them to bear this torture, and they even suffer themselves to be tied down while it is performing, in order that their agony may not interrupt the operator. The men commence tattooing as soon as they are able to bear the pain, generally at the age of eighteen or nineteen, and are rarely completely tattooed until they arrive at the age of thirty-five. The women begin about the same age, but have only their legs, arms, and hands tattooed, which is done with extraordinary neatness and delicacy. Some slight lines are drawn across their lips. It is also the practice with some to have the inside of their lips tattooed, but the object of this ornament I could never find out, as it is never seen unless they turn out their lips to show it. Every tribe in the island, I observed, was tattooed after a different fashion, and I was informed that every line had its meaning, and gave to the bearer certain privileges at their feasts. This practice of tattooing sometimes occasions sores which fester and are several weeks before they heal; it, however, never produces any serious consequences, or leaves any scars behind." Tattooing is practised now by all classes of seamen.

Here is a recent description of it which will interest the curious reader: "It is usually confined to the arms, hands, and occasionally to the breast, and we have known it to be thus performed. The design being first sketched on the skin with Indian ink, or charcoal, etc., the artist proceeds to delineate the same by means of needles, which are used singly, doubly, and trebly. The double and treble needles are lashed together with fine silk, the points being separated by passing the silk between them. With these tools, as with pencils of different degrees of fineness, the pictures are outlined and shaded; finally, by way of varnish, to bring the subject well out, a black, blue, or red mixture is rubbed in.

"Of course the devices vary according to the taste and feelings of the patient and the skill of the operator; thus the pangs of unrequited affection are soothed by hearts, and darts, and torches, bridal-wreaths, and true love-knots; professional taste is gratified by representations of ships, anchors, guns, swords, and the like; the mysteries of religion are denoted by devices of the cross and crucifix, and the sacred monogram I. H. S., together with the All-seeing eye; while a taste for the fine arts, combined with a love of pastoral life, is indicated by portraits of shepherds and shepherdesses, pipes—not tobacco—and crooks, lambs, and cottages.

"We proceed to describe a few specimens which have come under our own observation; and first we request attention to that dejected looking young sailor 'sighing like a furnace.' It is almost needless to mention that he is a victim to the tender passion, and in order to appease his sufferings the poor fellow has had pictured on his arm two hearts, the one large and the other small; beneath the hearts are two sets of initials, the whole surrounded by a nuptial wreath. The picture told its own tale; the hearts and the initials belonged to the lover and his betrothed; but to which of the two belonged the larger heart? There stands his messmate, apparently suffering from the same malady, but in a more intense degree.

Were it not for his jovial countenance we should deem his case desperate, for on his arm, below two crossed daggers, is delineated a bleeding heart pierced by a flaming dart.

"Next observe that staid old fellow; he has weathered 'the battle and the breeze' for many a long year. He is an upright and downright sort of man; and his taste being simple and chaste, his only adornment consists of a pair of punctured blue bracelets, relieved with red gems.

"In the month of June, 1856, we were watching a party of sailors belonging to the royal yacht Victoria and Albert. One of them evidently cherished domestic happiness, for he had the initials of all his family punctured up and down his arm, while on the back of his hand were sketched masonic emblems, the mysterious eye, the square, and the compasses. On the other arm, surrounded with arabesque ornaments, flourished a grim alligator; and to crown all, there appeared a pair of portraits of himself and his lady-love, or rather, not to be so sentimental, of 'the gal he left behind him.'

"On board the American steamship Niagara (June, 1857) we noticed one of her crew had on his arm the device of a cross standing on a pedestal, while on the horizontal arm of the cross a bleeding heart at one end balanced an anchor at the other.

"Here is a later example of the American type, in

the person 'of a man of color, who gave the name of Andrew Jackson Robinson, and said he had served in the Federal army.' He applied to the magistrate 'for relief in a state of great distress.' He explained that he deserted from the Forty-first regiment of Liberty Guards at the battle of Bull Run, and was afterwards caught and imprisoned in Fortress Monroe, from which he managed to escape and make his way to England in a vessel named the Charles Wesley, in the hold of which he had concealed himself. He bared his chest in the court to show that he was branded as a deserter, and was thus prevented obtaining employment in this country. He was also similarly branded on one hand. The Star-spangled Banner and other emblems of the American Union were elaborately tattooed in various colors on the skin, and covered the whole surface of his breast. He was shoeless, and without a coat. He said he did not know what on earth to do, for here he could get no work. He had been taken up for begging, and if he returned to America he would be liable to the conscription, if he escaped being shot as a deserter. Well, we may extend Christian charity even to a bad man—God help even the best of us if *worthiness* is to be the standard of acceptance! At all events, we may legitimately pity the fate of a poor fellow who was shipwrecked last winter on the coast of Cornwall, whose dead body was picked up near Zennor, and who, we trust, was identified, owing to his 'left arm being tattooed with a representation of a full-rigged ship, and a sailor having the English ensign over his shoulder.'

"Perhaps the reader would hardly expect to find the subject 'of man's first disobedience' illustrated on shipboard, and yet we saw a seaman belonging to the Queen's favorite little yacht, the Fairy, on whose arm was delineated Adam and Eve, looking the very incarnation of innocence. There they stood, one on each side of the Tree of Knowledge, listening to the appeal of the serpent, who was coiled round the trunk of the tree. 'The fruit of that forbidden tree' was so faithfully pictured in red, that one felt almost inclined to forgive 'the apple-eating traitress' for yielding to the temptation.

"During the month of August, 1845, we observed a seaman in Portsmouth dockyard who had a crucifix imprinted on his right arm, and on his left arm was neatly punctured the following verse:

'From rocks and sands and barren lands,
Kind fortune set me free;
From great guns and women's tongues
Good Lord deliver me!'

Observe the gallantry of the climax, which seems to imply that the noise of the artillery of women's tongues is more to be dreaded than the report of great guns."

Upon casting anchor in the bay off Madison's Island, a naked Englishman, in every thing but color like the natives, came to the ship. Many years he had been among the tropical islands, speaking their language, and conforming to all their customs; a man who was educated in a Christian land, changed to a savage, and proud to be a leader among them. Upon the hills of the island were companies of Indians presenting a strange and threatening aspect. It was discovered that a war was in progress between the people and a fighting tribe beyond the mountains. And as we shall have the brilliant victories of *Commodore* Farragut to narrate, we will take a partial view of the entirely new and exciting scenes of island warfare, which intensely enlisted the curiosity and awakened the enthusiasm of *Midshipman* Farragut.

The first thing which attracts attention is *the way* they fought. The hostile tribes assemble on the hill-tops, with the valley between them, when a warrior from one side advances in gay attire, ornamented with feathers, shells, and ear-pendants, dancing toward the enemy, and challenging to single combat. A shower of stones and spears welcomes the challenger, which he with marvellous dexterity avoids. He is then pursued by a large band of the enemy, who are in turn met and chased backward. If one is knocked down by a stone, the pursuers rush to the wounded man, and with spears and clubs soon despatch their victim, and then carry him away in triumph, each dipping his spear in the blood, which must not be wiped off but always remain, giving to the weapon the name of the dead warrior, and increasing its value. They used *slings* with great skill, which are made from the fibres of the cocoa-nut tree, and will throw a stone weighing half a pound. So powerful were these, that broken limbs, fractured skulls, and scars revealed the force and accuracy of their *sling-shots.* Their spears were sometimes weakened above the blade by holes, so as to break off and leave it in the body.

While the Essex was in communication with the natives on the shore, comprising three or four tribes, a camp was pitched, and a cannon with marines placed there. All the while the hostile Happahs from beyond the mountains lay along the summits, occasionally descending to the valleys, robbing the plantations, and exhibiting defiance toward the frigate. Captain Porter armed his men, and had a large gun removed to the base of the mountains by the friendly natives at war with the Happahs, who promised to convey it up the precipitous sides for battle, if our forces would join them there.

The Happahs were warned in vain, and seemed resolved to test the truth of their scornful declaration that the white strangers were cowards. While things were in this attitude, "an Indian girl," says the *general* of our little army, "who had been wandering in the bushes, came running toward us, the picture of fear, and with terror strongly marked in every feature, exclaimed that the Happahs were but a short distance from the camp. I directed the alarm gun to be fired; every person was immediately armed with such weapons as presented themselves, and we waited the expected attack behind our barrier, the water casks; but hearing no noise, we sallied out to examine the bushes, and supposed it a false alarm: but on returning to the camp, casting our eyes up the hills, we perceived a party skulking among the reeds and grass. We got the six-pounder to bear on them, soon dislodged them, and had no other interruption or alarm during the day.

"About eleven o'clock we perceived that our people had gained the mountains, and were driving the Happahs from height to height, who fought as they retreated, and daring our men to follow them with threatening gesticulations. A native, who bore the American flag, waved it in triumph as he skipped along the mountains. They were attended by a large concourse of friendly natives, armed as usual, who generally kept in the rear of our men. In about an hour we lost sight of the combatants, and saw no more of them until about four o'clock, when they were discovered descending the mountains on their return, the natives bearing five dead bodies, slung on poles."

For several days after victory and peace, the Essex remained among these pagans, whose ceremonies over the dead, and various customs, revealed the degradation of heathenism in contrast with Christianity, itself often disgraced in those morally dark lands by corrupt and wicked officials and their men from England and America.

Much, you know, has been done since that period by missionary societies in both countries to elevate the tribes of the Marquesas and kindred isles, where

> "Every prospect pleases,
> And only man is vile."

CHAPTER XI.

A Conspiracy—Rum—The Plot frustrated—The Island under the Stars and Stripes—The Typee War—Captain Porter's Defence of his Invasion—Native Customs and Island Scenes.

WHILE the Essex was lying at Madison's Island, so called by Captain Porter, but in the native dialect Nooaheevah, he discovered a conspiracy among his prisoners of war. Its object was to get possession of the Essex Junior, and then sail away from their captors. They had been allowed liberty to visit the shore freely by their magnanimous commander, on promise of good behavior. They took advantage of the indulgence, and matured their mutinous plans. At their head was Lawson, the mate of one of the prizes. The night of the 14th of November was appointed for the bold attempt to seize the vessel. A part of the plot was to mix laudanum with the rum drank by such of the crew as were not in the secret, reminding us of more recent attempts of our English friends to poison and destroy.

The vigilant officer in charge of the cruise narrates the remainder of the transaction, giving another instance of disobedience in which the necessity and the enforcement of law and order on board a man-of-war appears; also the formal possession of the island. "Lawson was to attend to the rum and laudanum. The third mate, with the prisoners on shore, was to get possession of the canoes on the beach, and with them surprise the ship and take her to sea, there being no other vessel ready to follow her, and no powder on board the Essex which would enable her to stop them. Such was their plan, and such their expectations. I had been informed of it almost as soon as it was conceived, was willing to humor the scheme, and gave them every opportunity of making the trial, adopting, at the same time, suitable means to have them secured and punished for their perfidy. At the time of the formation of this plan, and while Lawson and the others were using their greatest exertions to get rum at any price, our rum casks were lying on the gun-deck under charge of a sentinel, where they had been put while we were smoking the rats. Two of the sentinels were detected, one in conniving, and the other in assisting some persons in stealing rum. I did not inquire who were those concerned in the theft, lest the discovery might make known to the conspirators my knowledge of their scheme. I therefore punished the sentinels severely for not putting them to death; informed the crew generally of the most absolute necessity for extraordinary vigilance; and told the marines that for the next neglect of duty I should punish the offender to the utmost extent of my power.

"The next evening, after going my rounds at the camp, to see that every thing was right, I went to bed, and at half-past ten o'clock, not hearing the sentinel at the bakehouse call out 'All's well,' I inquired the cause. The sergeant of the guard, on examination, reported to me that the sentinel was lying down asleep, and that he had not disturbed him. I determined now, should this be the case, to punish him as he deserved. I felt the necessity of vigilance, not only on account of our prisoners, but on account of the natives. I felt persuaded that we owed the friendly footing on which we now stood with them entirely to our convincing them we were always on our guard, and I was determined that the safety of the whole should not be hazarded by the neglect of the marines. I therefore seized my pistol, and, followed by the sergeant and a guard, proceeded for the bakehouse, where we found the culprit fast asleep, his musket lying beside him. I directed him to be seized, and, at the same moment he was wounded through the fleshy part of the thigh. This example had a proper effect, and rendered every person more vigilant, particularly the marines. I shall make no further comments on this affair. If the punishment should appear a severe one, let those who censure me place themselves for a moment in my situation: I was far distant from the means of obtaining a judicial inquiry into his offence, which would probably have terminated fatally for him; promptness and vigilance on my part were the only sure guarantees to the success of a cruise so highly important to the interests of my country.

"As I before observed, Sunday night was the period fixed on by the conspirators for making their attempt. But unfortunately (or rather fortunately) for them, it so happened that a ship hove in sight off the mouth of the harbor on Saturday afternoon, and, on discovering us, stood off to sea under a press of sail. The Essex Junior immediately slipped her cables and gave chase to her, and not expecting her back before Monday, I put all my prisoners in irons, and thus at once frustrated a scheme which had wholly engrossed them for the last week. With a determination that I would make them suffer for violating their parole, I sent them all on shore to the village, and set them to work in building a wall to surround it, which was finished before my departure from the island.

"Another very disagreeable event occurred. Robert Dunn, quartermaster, had been threatened by the officer of the watch with punishment for some neglect of duty. Dunn said that the time for which he enlisted had expired, and if he was punished he would never again do duty in the ship. When this was reported to me, it occasioned me much uneasiness. Most of my crew were in the situation of Dunn, and it became necessary to find a remedy for the evil. Promptness and decision were indispensable, and with as little loss of time as possible I caused all hands to be called on the quarter-deck, where I informed them of the offence of Dunn. Then directing him to strip, I assured him that I should punish him severely, and, to prevent his ever doing duty in the ship, I should turn him on shore on the island; observing that his time was out, and it was proper he should have his discharge. After this, addressing myself to the ship's company, I expostulated with them on the impropriety and the evils likely to result from such conduct as Dunn's, and expressed a determination to have no man under my command who had it in his power to say his time was out, and he would no longer do duty. I informed them that the times of many were out, and from that moment I gave up all claim on them for their services; that they were their own masters, and should have their discharge on the spot. If they wished to enlist again for the cruise, I would enlist them, give them the usual advance, and, on a suitable occasion, give them three days' liberty on shore. That such as refused to enlist, but would bind themselves to do duty, might remain on board till I would have an opportunity of putting them on shore in some civilized place. They should be supplied with provisions, but should be allowed neither pay nor prize-money. Such as wished their discharge were called on for their names, in order that it might be made out in form, and they were all informed that the shipping papers were laid open for all such as wished to enter. I now was about proceeding to the punishment of Dunn, when most of the officers, petty officers, and seamen, came forward and solicited his pardon, stating that he appeared intoxicated at the time he made the observation, and not sensible of the offence he committed. Dunn also begged forgiveness most earnestly, and hoped, whatever other punishment I might inflict, I would not turn him on shore. He was sensible his offence had been a great one, but pleaded intoxication, and as a proof of his attachment to the ship, requested his name to be placed first on the list. I thought it on the whole advisable to pardon him; the men were all dismissed; every man of all the ships reëntered except one, who, from some foolish whim, did not wish to reënlist, although he was desirous of remaining, doing duty, and receiving pay. I determined not to depart from the principles laid down. I stopped his pay, and afterwards sent him to America in the New Zealander. This affair (which, when joined to conspiracies, neglect of duty, and my difficulties with the tribes, had caused me much uneasiness) was now settled.

"On the 19th November, the American flag was displayed in our fort, a salute of seventeen guns was fired from the artillery mounted there, and returned by the shipping in the harbor. The island was taken possession of for the United States, and called Madison's Island, the fort, Fort Madison, the village, Madisonsville, and the bay, Massachusetts Bay. The following declaration of the act of taking possession was read and signed, after which the prosperity of our newly-acquired island was drank by all present. The object of this ceremony had been previously and was again explained to the natives. They were all much pleased at being *Melleekees*, as they called themselves, and wanted to know if their new chief was as great a man as Gattanewa.

The peace with the natives enjoyed by the American cruisers was brief. The Typees, a powerful tribe, had made aggressions on the clans friendly to the people of the Essex, and even refused to contribute to it their share of supplies. To maintain his authority and influence with the chiefs who had given him their allegiance, the commander must bring the Typees to terms of honorable treatment of both parties insulted. Ambassadors were sent to them in vain; the only salutation was a shower of stones. The forces of the Essex then advanced with their allies into the thicket, where lay the Typees in ambuscade. "Snap, snap," went the slings, and the stones came whistling by, and at the same moment spears came whirling from the invisible foe. To retreat would create the impression of cowardice, and the only alternative was to march on and scour the woods. For a whole mile the brave fellows pressed forward in a continual tempest of these missiles, unharmed, when Lieutenant Downes fell with a broken leg. With an escort he was sent to the camp on the beach, and the warriors continued to advance. Then followed thrilling scenes of conflict in the tangled wild wood and swamps; the natives at last compelling the wounded and exhausted men of the Essex to retreat.

"The Essex's crew composed the main body, the rest being divided into scouting parties, headed by their respective officers. I directed the party sent in advance to halt as soon as they had gained the top of the mountain until I came up with the main body. There I intended encamping for the night, should our men not be able to stand the fatigue of a longer march. Several gave out before we reached the summit, which we did in about three hours, with great difficulty. But after resting a short time, and finding ourselves refreshed, the moon shining out bright, and our guides informing us (though very incorrectly) that we were not more than six miles from the enemy, we again marched. Several Indians had joined us, but I had imposed silence on them, as we were under the necessity of passing a Happah village, and was fearful of their discovering us, and giving intelligence to the Typees, Not a whisper was heard from one end of the line to the other; our guides marched in front, and we followed in silence up and down the steep sides of rocks and mountains, through rivulets, thickets, and reed brakes, and by the sides of precipices which sometimes caused us to shudder."

What a wildly romantic moonlight march! After many perilous adventures, hard marches, and severe battles, the men of the Essex so far subdued the Typees that peace was made with them, and nearly a *thousand hogs* were brought in and presented to the brave commander of the little fleet. It was a curious spectacle—those wild Indians with their simple flags, coming over the hills in all directions, and driving the *peace-offerings* before them.

The pearl-oyster hooks and the fishing, the delicious fruits, and beauty of the natives in their simple, natural life, compared with those of other islands, degraded by the vices of the white man, and the *foolish* religious observances of these heathens, all occupied the leisure of the crew, and made impressions on the younger minds which the lapse of years could not efface. For at that time but little was known of the distant isles, and the most of our information now is derived from the lips and pens of our intelligent, devoted missionaries, who have since visited almost every pagan land.

CHAPTER XII.

Departure from Madison's Island—Arrival at Valparaiso—Scenes in the Harbor—Unexpected appearance of the Enemy's Ships—Correspondence—Disregard of Neutrality Laws—The Battle—Midshipman Farragut a Hero in the Fight—Is Wounded—Captain Porter's Escape.

THE singular and not unmusical voices of the seamen while lifting the anchor echoed from the bow of the Essex, on the beautiful 9th of December, 1812, giving notice of departure from the pleasant shores of sunny islands. And now came the trial of restraint which was severely felt by the people of the Essex. Their freedom, which had been so great and protracted, was suddenly taken away, and there was a threatening discontent on the part of many. Soon the able commander quelled the rising insubordination by putting into a canoe and sending ashore White, the leader, and telling him never to let his face be seen again. Such is the unquestioned authority on board of a ship; no monarchy is more absolute. A poor Otaheitan who belonged to the crew, was struck by a boatswain, an indignity which he could not bear, and, shedding a flood of tears, he jumped overboard, saying no one should ever give him another blow. He was really mourned by all, for he was gentle and kind, and amused the "young gentlemen" especially with his imitations of the dancing customs and other peculiarities of his race.

The voyage for a month was off the coast of Chili, with no incidents of importance till the frigate reached Valparaiso, early in February, on the lookout for the enemy. The people in port were lavish in their hospitalities, as they were on the former visit of the Essex, and Captain Porter felt that he must reciprocate the attentions. On the 7th the guests from the city were on the Essex, and, as on the night before the battle of Waterloo,

"And all went merry as a marriage bell."

The awnings were up, and the flags, with various decorations, were fluttering in the midnight breeze. Suddenly a signal from the Essex Junior arrested the attention of the men of the Essex. Two hostile ships were in sight! There was "hurrying to and fro" on the decks of the frigate. "Boom!" went the signal-gun to call the seamen who were ashore to their carronades. When the sun was up the Englishmen were approaching the Essex, whose decks were "cleared for action." The Phœbe, a frigate, was commanded by Captain Hillyar, and her consort was the Cherub. The British commander and the American had often met in friendly social relations in other ports, but now there was the appearance of hostile intentions, although in a neutral harbor.

The Phœbe, with astonishment, saw that her antagonist was ready for an attack.

Captain Porter said: "Captain Hillyar, my ship is perfectly ready for action, but I shall act only on the defensive."

Affecting a careless manner, he leaned over the quarter, and replied: "Oh, sir, I have no intention of getting on board of you."

Captain Porter said: "If you do fall on board of me there will be much blood shed."

Just then the jib-boom swept across the forecastle of the Essex, exposing the Phœbe to a raking fire, while not one of her guns could touch her enemy. This was too *near* for a peaceful design.

The men of the Essex were summoned to board the British frigate. It was now a moment of the greatest consternation on the Phœbe. Her officers and crew saw the whole force of the Essex standing before them, armed, each with a cutlass and brace of pistols, while it was supposed the festive scene of the night had put the ship into complete disorder.

Captain Hillyar, more vehemently than ever, raising his hands, exclaimed: "Oh, sir, I had not the slightest intention of boarding you; it is all an accident, sir, that my ship is taken aback."

The truth is, he was at the mercy of the Essex, which could have destroyed the Phœbe in fifteen minutes, and resorted to falsehood to save his fortunes. The honorable officer of the American frigate believed the assertion, and permitted Captain Hillyar to disentangle himself, and drift away, all the time exposed to the wasting fire of her magnanimous foe.

When Captain Porter went on shore, the officers of the Government met him with the salutation: "Captain, why did you let the opportunity for destroying your enemy pass? We expected to see short work made with him."

Said the hero, "I have always respected the neutrality of your port, and shall continue to do so."

His record of the affair is honorable to him, and sheds lustre on his name.

"Although subsequent events have proved that Captain Hillyar was incapable of a similar forbearance, I have never regretted, for a single moment, that I permitted him to escape, when, either by accident or design, he had placed himself entirely at my mercy. At no time during the engagement which took place afterwards, or since, would I have changed situations or feelings with that officer.

"Captain Hillyar and Captain Tucker, the day after

their arrival, paid me a visit at the house of Mr. Blanco, where I generally stayed while on shore. Their visit was soon returned, and a friendly intimacy established, not only between the commanders and myself, but the officers and boats' crews of the respective ships. No one, to have judged from appearances, would have supposed us to have been at war, our conduct toward each other bore so much the appearance of a friendly alliance. At our first interview, I took occasion to tell Captain Hillyar it was very important that I should know of him whether he intended to respect the neutrality of the port. He replied, with much emphasis and earnestness: '*You* have paid so much respect to the neutrality of the port, that I feel myself bound in honor to respect it.' I told him the assurance was sufficient, and that it would place me more at ease, since I should now no longer feel it necessary to be always prepared for action.

"In the course of this conversation I adverted to a flag he had hoisted, containing the following motto: 'God and country; British sailors' best rights; traitors offend both;' and asked him the object of it. He said it was in reply to my motto of 'free trade and sailors' rights,' which gave great offence to the British navy; whenever I hoisted that flag, he should not fail to hoist the other. I told him my flag was intended solely for the purpose of pleasing ourselves, and not to insult the feelings of others; that his, on the contrary, was considered as highly insulting in the light of an offset against ours; and that if he continued to hoist it, I should not fail to retort on him. The next day, this flag being hoisted, I displayed one bearing the motto of 'God, our Country, and Liberty—tyrants offend them.' Three cheers followed on the part of the crew of the Phœbe, which were returned from my ship. The thing was taken in good part by Captain Hillyar; we talked freely and good-humoredly of the object of his coming to that sea; the long hunt he had after me, and of my views in coming to Valparaiso. He asked me what I intended to do with my prizes; when I was going to sea; and various other inquiries were put and answered. I told him whenever he sent away the Cherub I should go to sea; that it would depend upon him altogether when I departed; that, having thus met him, I should seek an opportunity of testing the force of the two ships. I added, that the Essex being smaller than the Phœbe, I did not feel that I should be justified to my country for losing my ship, if I gave him a challenge; but if he would challenge me, and send away the Cherub, I would have no hesitation in fighting him.

"To these, and similar observations, Captain Hillyar would reply, that the results of naval actions were very uncertain: they depended on many contingencies, and the loss of a mast or a spar often turned the fate of the day. He observed, that notwithstanding the inferiority of my ship, still, if I could come to close quarters with her carronades, I should no doubt do great execution. On the whole, therefore, he should trust to circumstances to bring us together, as he was not disposed to yield the advantage of a superior force, which would effectually blockade me until other ships arrived, and, at all events, prevent my doing any further injury to the commerce of Britain. As regarded my prizes, I informed him they were only encumbrances to me, and I should take them to sea and destroy them the first opportunity. He told me I dared not do it while he was in sight. I replied, 'We shall see.'

"Finding Captain Hillyar determined to yield none of the advantages of his superior force, and being informed there were other ships bound into the Pacific Ocean in pursuit of me, I secretly resolved to take every means of provoking him to a contest with his single ship. The Cherub being quite near to the Essex, the respective crews occasionally amused themselves with singing songs, selecting those most appropriate to their situation and feelings. Some of these were of their own composition. The songs from the Cherub were better sung, but those of the Essex were more witty, and more to the point. The national tune of 'Yankee Doodle' was the vehicle through which the crew of the Essex, in full chorus, conveyed their nautical sarcasms; while 'The Sweet Little Cherub that sits up Aloft,' was generally selected by their rivals. These things were not only tolerated, but encouraged, by the officers, through the whole of the first watch of the calm, delightful nights of Chili; much to the amusement of the people of Valparaiso, and the frequent annoyance of the crew of the Cherub. At length Captain Hillyar requested me to put a stop to this practice, and I informed him I certainly should not do so while the singing continued on board the Cherub."

The escape of a prisoner, and his rescue from the sea into which he sprang from the Essex Junior, by the Phœbe, led to a spirited correspondence between the officers of the opposing frigates. Two of the letters I must quote, because they will again make you think of English and Canadian plottings with rebels in the great rebellion, and afford a further insight into the early culture of young Farragut in loyalty, magnanimity, and the right way to fight a desperate foe:

"His Britannic Majesty's Ship Phœbe,
Valparaiso, *9th Feb.*, 1814.

"Sir,—By an Englishman picked up by one of his Majesty's sloop Cherub's boats, in a drowning state, Captain Tucker has been informed that nine of our countrymen are suffering the miseries of close confinement on board the American ship of war under your orders; and that the calamity of imprisonment is aggravated by their being kept in irons. As this mode of treatment is so contrary to any I have ever witnessed during a very long servitude, as well as the usages of honorable warfare, may I beg (if the statement is just) that you will do me the favor to interest yourself in their behalf. I have the honor to be, &c.,

"(Signed) JAMES HILLYAR."

"U. S. FRIGATE ESSEX, VALPARAISO, *10th Feb.*, 1814.

"SIR,—I have the honor to acknowledge the receipt of your letter of yesterday. The information you have received from the prisoner who made his escape from my armed prize, and who was assisted in effecting it by the boat and crew of his Majesty's ship Cherub, is correct as respects the situation of the remaining prisoners of war on board the Essex Junior, as well as those in the frigate I have the honor to command.

"When at the Island of Nooaheevah, my prisoners, while on their parole of honor, made a most diabolical attempt to possess themselves of my prize by means of poison, with a view of making their escape. I detected and secured them; and when I no longer apprehended further danger, I liberated them. Since my arrival here, I have again found it necessary to secure them, and those on board my prize have been confined two days.

"I have not, perhaps, had as long a servitude as Captain Hillyar; nor was it necessary I should, to learn honor and humanity. I deem it only necessary to say, that, of the many prisoners who have fallen into my hands since hostilities commenced between the United

States and Great Britain, none have been confined but for my own security; or otherwise punished but when they deserved it. I have the honor to be, &c.,

"(Signed) D. PORTER."

The conduct of Captain Hillyar roused the indignation of Captain Porter, and he resolved to seek an engagement, and conquer or be conquered.

Notes passed between the commanders, and the American officer ordered the prize Hector towed out of the harbor and burned, on purpose to provoke a battle. In his report to the Secretary of the Navy the name of the boy Farragut, as we shall see, appears, intimating what was indeed true, that he was a veteran in the fight, fearing shot no more than he would snow balls, while pistol and cutlass had no terrors for him.

Wrote his captain: "The Phœbe, agreeably to my expectations, came to seek me at Valparaiso, where I was anchored with the Essex, my armed prize the Essex Junior, under the command of Lieutenant Downes, on the lookout off the harbor. But, contrary to the course I thought he would pursue, Commodore Hillyar brought with him the sloop-of-war Cherub, mounting twenty-eight guns, eighteen thirty-two pound carronades, eight twenty-fours, and two long nines on the quarter-deck and forecastle, and a complement of a hundred and eighty men. The force of the Phœbe is as follows: Thirty long eighteen-pounders, sixteen thirty-two pound carronades, one howitzer, and six three-pounders in the tops—in all fifty-three guns, and a complement of three hundred and twenty men; making a force of eighty-one guns and five hundred men. In addition to which, they took on board the crew of an English letter of marque lying in port. Both ships had picked crews, and were sent into the Pacific in company with the Raccoon of twenty-two guns, and a storeship of twenty guns, for the express purpose of seeking the Essex, and were prepared with flags bearing the motto, 'God and country; British sailors' best rights; traitors offend both.' This was intended as a reply to my motto, '*Free trade and sailors' rights*,' under the erroneous impression that my crew were chiefly Englishmen, or to counteract its effect on their own crews. The force of the Essex was forty-six guns—forty thirty-two pound carronades and six long twelves; and her crew, which had been much reduced by prizes, amounted only to two hundred and fifty-five men. The Essex Junior, which was intended chiefly as a storeship, mounted twenty guns, ten eighteen-pound carronades, and ten short sixes, with only sixty men on board. In reply to their motto I wrote at my mizzen—'*God, our Country, and Liberty—tyrants offend them.*'"

For six weeks the enemy lay off the port to blockade the Essex. Ineffectual efforts were made to close in decisive conflict. March 28th a gale parted the cable of the

Essex, and she drifted to sea, when a heavy squall carried away her main topmast. Thus crippled, the Phœbe and Cherub came upon her, but the boys worked the twelve-pounders with almost superhuman skill and courage, compelling the foe to retire after an hour of desperate encounter, in which several on both sides were killed and wounded. Soon after the vessels sprang at each other, the Englishman leading, like tigers from their lair; and flame, thunder, and smoke, were the signals of deadly strife, paving the decks with the slain, and filling the cockpit with the wounded. At last, unable to bring a gun to bear, the British fire raked mercilessly the Essex, mowing down the men at every discharge, and several times setting her on fire. It was a time to try the courage of all on board left alive. The magazine was threatened by the flames! Those who could swim were ordered to try for the shore, less than a mile distant. The remaining part of the crew *flew at the fires*, extinguished them, and then commenced firing at the foe again. In the thickest of the fight was Farragut, unconscious of the peril until drawn back by strong hands from his perilous position.

Records the heroic commander: "I was informed that the cockpit, the steerage, the wardroom, and the berth-deck could contain no more wounded; that the wounded were killed while the surgeons were dressing them, and that, unless something was speedily done to

The Battle in the Bay of Valparaiso, p. 176.

prevent it, the ship would soon sink from the number of shot-holes in her bottom; and, on sending for the carpenter, he informed me that all his crew had been killed or wounded, and that he had been once over the side to stop the leaks, when his slings had been shot away, and it was with difficulty he was saved from drowning. The enemy, from the smoothness of the water and the impossibility of our reaching him with our carronades, and the little apprehension that was excited by our fire, which had now become much slackened, was enabled to take aim at us as at a target: his shot never missed our hull, and my ship was cut up in a manner which was, perhaps, never before witnessed; in fine, I saw no hopes of saving her, and at twenty minutes after six P. M. gave the painful order to strike the colors. Seventy-five men, including officers, were all that remained of my whole crew, after the action, capable of doing duty, and many of them severely wounded, some of whom have since died. *The enemy still continued his fire*, and my brave though unfortunate companions were still falling about me. I directed an opposite gun to be fired, to show them we intended no further resistance; *but they did not desist; four men were killed at my side, and others in different parts of the ship.* I now believed he intended to show us no quarter, and that it would be as well to die with my flag flying as struck, and was on the point of again hoisting it, when about *ten minutes after hauling the colors down he ceased firing!*

8*

"I cannot speak in sufficiently high terms of the conduct of those engaged for such an unparalleled length of time (under such circumstances) with me in the arduous and unequal contest. Let it suffice to say, that more bravery, skill, patriotism, and zeal, were never displayed on any occasion. Every one seemed determined to die in defence of their much loved country's cause, and nothing but views to humanity could ever have reconciled them to the surrender of the ship; they remembered their wounded and helpless shipmates below. The conduct of that brave and heroic officer, acting lieutenant John G. Cowel, who lost his leg in the latter part of the action, excited the admiration of every man in the ship, and after being wounded would not consent to be taken below, until loss of blood rendered him insensible. Mr. Edward Barnewell, acting sailing-master, whose activity and courage were equally conspicuous, returned on deck after his first wound, and remained after receiving his second until fainting with loss of blood. Mr. Samuel B. Johnson, who had joined me the day before, and acted as marine officer, conducted himself with great bravery, and exerted himself in assisting at the long guns, the musketry after the first half hour being useless from our great distance.

"Mr. M. W. Bostwick, whom I had appointed acting purser of the Essex Junior, and who was on board my ship, did the duties of aid in a manner which reflects on him the highest honor, and midshipmen Isaacs, Farragut, and Ogden, as well as acting midshipmen James Terry, James R. Lyman, and Samuel Duzenbury, and master's mate William Pierce, exerted themselves in the performance of their respective duties, and gave an earnest of their value to the service. The first three are too young to recommend for promotion; the latter I beg leave to recommend for confirmation, as well as the acting lieutenants, and Messrs. Barnewall, Johnson, and Bostwick.

"We have been unfortunate, but not disgraced; the defence of the Essex has not been less honorable to her officers and crew than the capture of an equal force; and I now consider my situation less unpleasant than that of Commodore Hillyar, who, in violation of every principle of honor and generosity, and regardless of the rights of nations, attacked the Essex in her crippled state within pistol shot of a neutral shore—when, for six weeks, I had daily offered him fair and honorable combat, on terms greatly to his advantage. The blood of the slain must be on his head, and he has yet to reconcile his conduct to heaven, to his conscience, and to the world. To possess the Essex it cost the British Government near six millions of dollars, and yet her capture was owing entirely to accident."

Captain Porter compliments highly the ladies of Valparaiso, who, while the authorities were negligent, were unwearied in their attention to his wounded heroes; angels of mercy, conveying, in their own hands, the wounded to the hospital provided, and then watching over them in their sufferings. Many lives were saved by this timely and tender care.

Not knowing what to do with his captives, Captain Hillyar decided to make a cartel of the Essex Junior and send them home. Captain Porter with his crew sailed for New York, and, when off Sandy Hook, was hailed by the British ship-of-war Saturn, Captain Nash, who, in violation of all right in the case, determined to retain the Essex Junior and her men, making them prisoners of war. The injured, magnanimous hero of the Pacific voyage and battle, shall tell the rest of the story of his homeward sail:

"At seven the next morning, the wind being light from the southward, and the ships about thirty or forty miles off the eastern part of Long Island, within about musket shot of each other, I determined to attempt my escape. There appeared no disposition on the part of the enemy to liberate the Essex Junior, and I felt myself justified in this measure. A boat was accordingly lowered down, manned and armed, and I left with Lieutenant Downes the following message for Captain Nash: 'That Captain Porter was now satisfied that most British officers were not only destitute of honor, but regardless of the honor of each other; that he was armed, and prepared to defend himself against his boats, if sent in pursuit of him; and that he must be met, if met at all, as an enemy.' I now pulled off from the ship, keeping the Essex Junior in a direct line between my boat and the Saturn, and got nearly gunshot from her before they discovered me. At that instant a fresh breeze sprang up, and the Saturn made all sail after us. Fortunately, however, a thick fog came on, upon which I changed my course, and entirely eluded further pursuit. During the fog I heard a firing, and on its clearing up saw the Saturn in chase of the Essex Junior, which vessel was soon brought to. After rowing and sailing about sixty miles, I at last succeeded, with much difficulty and hazard, in reaching the town of Babylon, on Long Island, where, being strongly suspected of being a British officer, I was closely interrogated; and, my story appearing rather extraordinary, was not credited. But on showing my commission all doubts were removed, and from that moment all united in affording me the most liberal hospitality. On my arrival by land at New York, the reception given me by the inhabitants, as well as by those of every other place through which I passed, it becomes not me to record. It is sufficient to say, it has made an impression on my mind never to be effaced.

"The Essex Junior, after being detained the whole of the day following my escape, and ransacked for money; her crew mustered on deck, under pretence of detecting deserters; her officers insulted, and treated with shameful outrage; was at length dismissed, and arrived next day at New York, where she was condemned and sold."

No heart could be more tried and indignant amid all these scenes of outrage to his kind commander and to himself, still bearing his wound from British weapons, than Midshipman Farragut's—one of the "middies" at that time in the United States navy. We find in an old Boston almanac his name entered "Glasgow Farragut"—no middle name, and a single R in the last. How he was afterwards welcomed to Boston, from whose harbor he had sailed unknown, we shall learn.

CHAPTER XIII.

Midshipman Farragut returns to the United States—A Good Story—Enters the Military School at Chester—Again at Sea—The Chaplain his Friend—At Tunis with the Consul—Historic Scenes—Development of Character—Afloat again—At Norfolk—Marriage—Promotion.

ALTHOUGH Farragut landed in New York without his commander, and while he was drifting and moving about in a small craft, they reached the metropolis safely, and not far apart in time. Again the young Catalonian was restored to his *paternal* officer, who, after receiving the most enthusiastic demonstrations of admiration from his countrymen, was again put in command.

A good story has been current about our hero-boy, the exact truth of which cannot be verified; but it is so like the young adventurer that it will bear reading. The President sailed from New York just before the Essex did, and was taken by the Endymion the middle of January, 1813. Still, such an incident may have occurred after his return, repeating the reckless, heroic daring of the fight at Valparaiso.

"The British man-of-war Plantagenet, seventy-four guns, fell in with the cruiser President, off Charleston, South Carolina. The President being much inferior to the Plantagenet, both in men and guns, her commander did not think it right to risk a battle with the Englishman; and so he crowded all sail to escape her by running into the harbor. This, of course, encouraged the Plantagenet to chase. The wind being fair, both ships were soon rapidly nearing the bar. The commander of the President knew that the Englishman drew too much water to get in, and felt confident that the ship could, if the tide served. Just as he had made up his mind to run boldly in, the wind died away, leaving both ships nearly becalmed almost within gunshot of each other. Then, while trying to coax enough wind into his sails to carry his ship to the bar, the American determined to send Midshipman Farragut in a boat to sound the channel. The boat was called away, and left the ship with little Farragut, then about fifteen years old, seated grimly in the stern, with his hand on his sword and his eye on the bar.

"Imagine the little fellow's consternation, when, looking back, he saw his ship making all sail toward the Plantagenet with a freshening breeze, while he could distinctly hear the call to quarters. The wind had shifted and grown quite fresh, cutting the President off from all chance of getting into Charleston harbor, and her captain at once determined to attack the Englishman boldly. And thus it happened that the little midshipman, Farragut, stood stamping his tiny feet in rage of disappointment, while the President sailed away from him to fight the Plantagenet.

" 'I'll be on board to fight the Plantagenet yet!' quoth Farragut. 'I will, I will! Set the sails, men! Be alive—be alive! Don't stand with your mouths open!'

" 'Please, sir,' said the cockswain, 'this boat is very crank, sir, and the breeze is fresh, sir. I know she'll go over if we do.'

" 'Set the sail!' cried Farragut; 'I'll be on board before that ship takes the Plantagenet, or drown you all!'

" The sail was set, and the little boat began to plough through the water.

" Said Farragut: 'Wet the sail, men, and don't lose an inch! What fine fat hams and pet pigs those Englishmen have! a good time we'll have to-morrow in our mess! We'll take this fellow before night!'

" Just then a squall struck the boat, and into the water went Midshipman Farragut with his boat's crew.

" 'Oh! what will the captain say to me for upsetting the boat, and losing the oars and tackle; and I've lost the fight too!' cried Farragut, as his head came up out of the water.

" He began to sneeze the salt water out of his eyes

and nose, as he looked round at the men's heads popping up, one by one, out of the waves.

"'It's bad enough to lose the tackle; and now you've not only lost the fight for me, but you want to drown yourselves too. I'll kill the first man that dares to drown!' and little Farragut sputtered and scolded away at the men to keep afloat, until they got on the bottom of his boat, where he bewailed his fate in missing the action.

"The result, however, was different from what every one expected. When the captain of the Plantagenet saw the President intended to fight him, he suddenly changed his course, and absolutely ran away, much to the satisfaction of all, particularly Farragut, who was picked off of the bottom of his boat in a short time, wet and disconsolate. The Englishman, it was afterwards discovered, had declined to fight because his men were in a state of mutiny; and, upon his arrival at home, a court of inquiry justified him."

Upon the return of peace, in the autumn of 1814, Captain Porter secured for Farragut, whose promise of a successful career had been watched and appreciated by him, a place in a school at Chester, Penn., in which were taught the elementary tactics of the military and naval science. In this then quiet and ancient town on the banks of the Delaware, fourteen miles from Philadelphia, the midshipman passed a profitable year, when his love of the sea led him again to its familiar scenes. He was sent to the Mediterranean squadron, and his home was on board its flag-ship, Washington, seventy-four guns, under Commodore Isaac Chauncey, whose chaplain, Rev. Chas. Folsom, since professor in Cambridge University, became his instructor and friend. It was a crisis in his experience and career. The boy was passing into manly youth, and the cultivated taste and elevated sentiments of his teacher had a commanding influence over him, which he has ever since gratefully acknowledged. This was before naval schools were established, and candidates for the naval service were taught on board the ships. A large number were committed to Mr. Folsom. For two years the relation of preceptor and student continued ripening into a mutual affection. And when, upon leaving his post, Mr. Folsom was appointed consul to Tunis, it was arranged that Farragut should have a furlough and accompany him.

In regard to this arrangement Mr. Folsom says: "I describe him as he now appeared to me by one word, 'ARIEL.' Our mutual joy was complete. The intent was, that I should be literally 'his guide, philosopher, and friend,' acting according to my own discretion, but officially accountable for him as his superior officer (for I had not resigned my place in the navy). While clothed with this complete authority, I do not remember that I ever issued an 'order,' or had occasion to make a suggestion that amounted to a reproof. All needed control was that of an elder over an affectionate younger brother."

Life in Tunis was entirely new. Young Farragut went from his retired, rural home, to sea, on whose bosom he had lived, with the exception of holidays in port, and the brief period in school at Chester, excluded from the highest social influence, and familiar intercourse with educated people. But in addition to his fraternal mentor, he was introduced to the best and most varied aspects of refined society, which can be found only where the consulates of the old European nations, and of the New World also, are established; and from the character of the surroundings, bring frequently the representatives of foreign courts and their families together. Mr. Folsom's *protége* was at once welcomed to this focus of aristocratic associations and splendor—not to be *spoiled*, but to see the world as he had not before, and feel the intellectual stimulus of contact with so much talent and culture.

The American consul assures us that his "young countryman was the delight of old and young. This had always been among his chief moral dangers; but here he learned to be proof against petting and flattery. Here, too, he settled his definition of true glory—glory, the idol of his profession—if not in the exact words of Cicero, at least in his own clear thought. Our familiar walks and rides were so many lessons in ancient history; and the lover of historical parallels will be gratified to know that we possibly sometimes stood on the very spot where the boy Hannibal took the oath that consecrated him to the defence of his country."

The city and kingdom of Tunis offered much to attract and intensely interest the youthful Farragut. There was first of all the ancient historical glory of the state. Ten miles to the northwest of the modern city of Tunis is the site of ancient Carthage, the famous metropolis of antiquity, founded by Queen Dido, nearly a thousand years before the advent of Christ. Here lived Hannibal, who, when he was nine years old, at his father's command, swore on the altar of his deity eternal hatred to the Romans; and when twenty-six, went forth at the head of an army, to redeem the vow. He had at one time forty elephants with his more than one hundred thousand troops.

Carthage was called a republic, but quite unlike our own in extent, and in both civil or religious life. The ruins are now chiefly the remains of moles, and of a magnificent aqueduct built by the Romans after their conquest. Among these relics of past heroism and glory the young midshipman wandered with his classic guide, musing over the departed greatness of the splendid commercial emporium—the queen of northern Africa.

To stand where Hannibal issued words of command, where the Roman generals rode proudly at the head of invading armies—to read over the story of Virgil there, was a thrilling and memorable experience. It colored all subsequent thought, and moulded destiny. Nor was Tunis wanting in objects to engage attention, although the streets are irregular and filthy. The palace of the bey is the principal edifice, where is enthroned absolute power. The court-room is a display of it in obsequious and gaily attired officials, while the guilty tremble before the unalterable decisions of unquestioned authority. The houses of the consuls resemble *prisons*, and stand apart from the rest of the dwellings, which are of one story, having flat roofs, with their cisterns for catching rain-water. The bazaars along the street display fabrics and perfumes of every kind.

It is not difficult to imagine the familiar talks of Farragut, then seventeen, and the consul, who made a companion of the high-minded, manly youth. Thus swiftly vanished a year, when the signals of a tropical pestilence were seen spreading terror on every hand. No official duty required the midshipman to stay amid its dangers, and with a tearful adieu he joined a Danish family and journeyed to Italy, where he again connected himself with the naval service on the Mediterranean. Amid the routine of duties on shipboard in time of peace he pursued his studies, carrying out, practically, the noble impulse he received in his career, under the care of Mr. Folsom.

January 1st, 1821, he received the appointment of

lieutenant in the navy, and was ordered to join the squadron in the West Indies. No stirring events marked his official service for the three years which followed. He was a gentleman, and in all his bearing displayed refinement of feeling, and a marvellous freedom from any taint of foreign intercourse with the licentious pagan and aristocratic European. He was next sent to Norfolk navy yard, remaining there till 1832. This port of entry, in a county of the same name, is situated on the northeast side of the Elizabeth River, eight miles above its mouth, thirty-two miles from the ocean, one hundred and twelve from Richmond, and two hundred and twenty-nine from Washington. Its streets are crooked, and the buildings not elegant. The country around is low, and in some places marshy. The hospitality of the citizens has always been noted. The harbor is a beautiful basin, about a mile in width, and was defended by three forts—Norfolk, Nelson, and that on Craney Island. A mile from the town, between the east and west branches of the river, was a marine hospital, and on the opposite side, a little further up, is the village of Gosport, the site of the navy yard. Here Farragut passed another crisis in his history memorable in the experience of ripening manhood. He married Miss Loyall, the daughter of a prominent citizen of Norfolk. She soon became a hopeless invalid. The years of suffering which she knew was only another trial of character, which, like the cataract's break in the current, revealing forms of beauty, and making a deeper, broader channel below, not only brought out the fine qualities of the man, but gave a wide range of thought and feeling, more strength and force, to his noble nature. He was affectionate and faithful until death came to the relief of the sufferer. He was a sincere mourner at the grave of the departed.

July, 1832, Lieutenant Farragut was ordered to the Vandalia, cruising off the coast of Brazil. Upon his return he was again stationed at Norfolk. Here he married Miss Virginia Loyall, sister of the former Mrs. Farragut. Their only son, LOYALL FARRAGUT, is a cadet in the Military Academy at West Point; and who will not watch with peculiar interest the record of the representative of a father so *loyal*, and so beloved by the nation?

Again in 1837 we find our admiral afloat, having been appointed executive officer, or lieutenant commander, of the war-sloop Natchez, of the West India squadron. In November, 1840, his post of official duty was once more at Norfolk till February of the next year, when, in the seventy-four gunship Delaware, he sailed to the coast of Brazil. In September he was commissioned commander —the grade next above that of lieutenant—a merited progress in the regular line of promotion, whose highest place of honor was waiting for him. While off Brazil, he was detached from the Delaware and put in command of the sloop-of-war Decatur.

These voyages of the peaceful cruisers had but little to interest besides the tropical scenery and fruits, and intercourse with officers of the foreign nations. *Bathing* in the warm latitudes is often made the scene of excitement by the cry of "*A shark! A shark!*" which soon dies away in the hurrah following the escape, or in the sadness attending the tragical fate of the incautious seaman. Brazil is always interesting to the traveller. Its grand rivers and mountains, its magnificent foliage, its brilliant birds and flowers, cannot fail to beguile the hours of a visit to its shores.

Commander Farragut reached Norfolk February 24th, 1843, when he was detached from the Decatur and granted leave of absence, a furlough intensely enjoyed in the quieter experience of a citizen; for, from boyhood a sailor, he had been for almost the whole period a stranger to the business and enjoyments which belong to life on shore. At Tunis, he was at a consulate in a strange land; at Norfolk navy yard, associated still with the service of the marine.

April 17th, 1844, the receiving ship Pennsylvania, at Norfolk, became the domain of Farragut's command. The superintendence of its affairs, the coming and going of the seamen, required that good executive management which has always characterized our vice-admiral. The following year his service was again in the navy yard.

His next position of honor and usefulness was the

command of the sloop-of-war Saratoga, of the home squadron, cruising in the West Indies, to which he was appointed March 9th, 1847.

March 3d, 1848, he was detached from this service, and April 10th was again at Norfolk. On the 29th of that month he was detached to await orders; another interlude of rest and leisure, but not of idleness or dissipation. The culture of Farragut's mind was uninterrupted during all the years of varied duty.

March 15th, 1851, he was called to Washington as inspector of ordnance; and a year later he was removed to Norfolk in the same service. For three years he might have been seen walking the rounds of business, among the grim servants of war, unconsciously keeping them in readiness for rebel hands, ere long to be lifted against the life of the republic.

Farragut was then ordered (August 9th, 1854) to California, in charge of the Man Island navy yard. It was opened for the Pacific coast, which the discovery of gold had made a new empire of commercial wealth and activity under the flag of the republic. This was six years after the precious metal was found in the sands of a mill-race, while Lieutenant Sherman was there in the United States service, and a spectator of the great event. In September of the succeeding year, the next step in the march of legitimate and worthy advancement was taken, by Commander Farragut's promotion to a captaincy in the navy—the highest position of authority on a single ship. Having retired from the navy yard on the Pacific coast May 29th, 1858, on New Year's day he was ordered to the Brooklyn, a noble sloop-of-war of the home squadron. In this position the political campaign of 1860 found him. He watched the issue with intense solicitude; for, though a Southerner by birth and marriage, he loved the old flag with a devotion second to that of no man in the land. Whatever the result, he was resolved to stand by the Stars and Stripes.

For nearly fifty years Captain Farragut had been in the naval service or on furlough only. Nineteen years had been spent on the sea. In the comparatively unexciting course of official duties he was a diligent student and careful observer. While abroad, he had learned the Turkish and Arabic, and was also familiar with many other tongues. It was a remarkable instance of long and thorough preparation for a crowning work in the country's cause, that would place his name among the first, if not the very first, on the roll of naval commanders and heroes. He did not, could not know the design of Providence; content to make the most of his official position for the national honor, and of his time in varied experience and mental culture. Upright, genial, modest, and devout, he, like our Grant, was God's man for the coming hour of terrible conflict and national peril.

CHAPTER XIV.

The Civil War opens—Norfolk—Captain Farragut—Exciting Scenes—Patriotic Words—Leaves Norfolk—Escape North—His New Home—Offers himself to the Country—Naval Expeditions—The Blockade.

AT four o'clock on Friday, April 12th, the sound of cannon in Charleston harbor awoke thousands of sleepers, who hastened toward the strange and exciting scene, and looked upon the smoke and flame which signalled the fate of the fair lands of the "Sunny South," although her exulting despots knew it not.

At that moment the State Convention of Virginia was deliberating upon the question of secession in Richmond. To secure Union delegates from his district, Captain Farragut, whose residence was in Norfolk, had counselled and labored, spending the whole night in the political meetings which appointed them. He hoped and expected that Virginia would maintain her fealty to the Government. But on the 17th the ordinance of secession was passed by a vote of 88 in favor, and 55 against it. Sumter had fallen, and the "Old Dominion" also. Captain Farragut was sad, but, with his noble and equally loyal wife, he felt no hesitation in regard to *his* course. He warned the people against the horrors of civil revolution, which his varied experience in foreign countries had shown him was blighting to all that is valuable to the State. They laughed at him, calling him an "old croaker."

April 19th, 1861, the Northern troops were fired upon by the mob of Baltimore, baptizing with blood, on that anniversary day of the first Revolutionary slaughter, the civil conflict. Captain Farragut saw about him the scowling emissaries of treason, plotting the further seizure of the public property. They invited and urged him to join them in the foul and malignant conspiracy, and with them strike for Southern rights. He listened to their dark designs, enforced by appeals to his ambition, domestic ties, and earliest, warmest associations.

"You are by birth and natural sympathies with us; and any position in the Confederacy you may desire will be yours."

Such was the pleading, heard with quickening pulse. They had discerned the lion of battle slumbering beneath the gentle exterior, and sought his power for their unholy cause. His loyal heart beat indignantly; and though pure in morals and religious in spirit, he could find utterance in no common forms of speech. Pointing to the national colors, with flashing eye, and face all aglow with the patriotic protest against their wickedness, with no thought of profanity, he exclaimed:

"Gentlemen, I tell you I would see every man of yor *damned, before I would raise my arm against that flag!*"

"Then, sir, you will not be permitted to stay here," was the bitter reply.

"I will seek some place where I can live, and on two hours' notice;" was the unhesitating response of the loyal captain.

He repaired to his residence, and informed his family that immediate preparations must be made to bid farewell to Norfolk. The afternoon and evening was a time of gloom, and yet of activity which had the air of cheerfulness, because loyalty was its inspiration. The next morning, April 18, 1861, Captain Farragut passed out of the city, with his face toward the north; carrying with him a few valuables from the arena of treasonable plots, and the consciousness of a pure and lofty purpose.

Crossing the Potomac, he stopped at the house of a friend. Scarcely had the salutations been exchanged, before he said: "Mr. ——, I am here without money, or place where I can lay my head."

When he reached Baltimore the mob ruled the city, and he barely succeeded in getting passage by steamer and canal boat to Columbia, Pennsylvania; thence on the railroad to New York. Meanwhile, Saturday night, April 21st, there was quite a different scene from his unknown arrival in the peaceful metropolis, near his former post of duty and his place of abode. To save the navy yard there from the hands of the rebels, it became necessary to destroy it. As the Sabbath began to dawn, the mines and combustibles were ready. The Pawnee and Cumberland floated away from the doomed spot, and sent up the signal rocket to fire the tinder-covered and costly structures. Immediately followed the grand and awful conflagration, till the navy yard was a plain of smouldering ruins.

The news of the terrific change which had already come over Norfolk since he left its old and familiar streets, found him busy with plans to secure a peaceful refuge for his family. The green valleys of the glorious Hudson attracted his steps; and the lovely village of Hastings, twenty miles from the city, was selected for his northern home.

He now returned to Washington, to offer his services to the nation assailed by the propagandists of slavery.

The navy of the United States was scattered abroad, through the traitorous management of the Buchanan Secretary, who anticipated the collision between the North and South, and in this department of the Government weakened it as much as possible. There was no vacant position in the service for the patriotic captain. But unwilling to lose the opportunity of securing him for the national cause, the Government gave him a seat in the Naval Retiring Board. This honorable but not pleasant duty was to sift out unworthy officers, and promote the loyal and worthy. Meanwhile the civil war had deepened in awful importance, and widened in extent.

In July bloody Manassas thrilled, depressed, then thoroughly aroused the country to the magnitude of the struggle. The beautiful village of Hampton, near Fortress Monroe, was burned by the rebels—the first torch of the kind lighting up the field of conflict—its flames rising over an unarmed, unoffending people.

The latter part of August, the first secret naval expedition, including the Minnesota, Wabash, Pawnee, Monticello, and Harriet Lane, war-steamers, sailed with transports from Hampton Roads for Hatteras Inlet, to take the rebel forts erected there, and hold the key of Albermarle Sound. Commodore Stringham commanded the sea forces, and General Butler those of the land. The splendid success of the expedition we all know. After a protracted and terrible bombardment, the white flag was raised on the walls of Fort Hatteras.

The next grand move in the naval field of action was under Dupont in October, 1861, whose fleet consisted of eighteen men-of-war and thirty-eight transports; the latter carrying troops for the land attack. Port Royal was the destination of the *armada*. The guarding forts were

Beauregard and Walker, which the rebels thought were impregnable, till the fleet rained its ponderous iron hail and exploding shells upon the garrisons. The terrified enemy made their escape. Among the heroes of this battle was William H. Steel, only fourteen years of age, who handed up powder for one of the guns, amid the fiery hail and flying fragments, as coolly as a veteran of three score years could have done.

January, 1862, a third maritime expedition was fitted out, Commodore Goldsborough commanding, and General Burnside leading the land forces. The splendid fleet moved from Hampton Roads, while a host of admiring spectators watched the grand march of the seventy ships, with banners in the breeze, and bands of music beneath the starry ensigns.

Off Cape Hatteras a terrific gale scattered the fleet. Amid the awful dash and roar of the billows, General Burnside was calm in his trust; "feeling," he said, "that God held them in the hollow of his hand."

February 8th, saw the victorious charge on Park Point battery, followed by the capture of Roanoke Island and Newbern. A month later, the Monitor and the Merrimac met at Hampton Roads, and the "Yankee Cheese Box" sent the rebel monster limping to his guarded den.

Fort Pulaski was added, early in April, to the bombarded and conquered strongholds of the rebellion.

At the same moment a magnificent naval expedition

was in progress, whose success was to send the name of Farragut around the world, with applause.

We will close this chapter with a stirring poem, which furnishes a vivid glimpse of the blockading work during the war, along our extended coast.

THE BLOCKADE.

Our ship is steaming o'er the wave,
Off Carolina's sandy shore,
The new moon, silent as the grave,
In crescent form is hanging o'er.

Along the rim of clouds that lower,
Where heaven and ocean seem to meet,
The lightning plays in wondrous power,
Illuming far the watery sheet.

Anon its flashes disappear,
And darker grows the gathering cloud,
While God's own fearful voice we hear—
In thunder—rolling deep and loud.

From Bald-Head * like a blazing star,
A light gleams seaward, far and near;
Beyond the reef and sandy bar
Appears the river channel clear.

The moon descends beneath the deep,
And still our vessel rides the sea;
And still the lurid lightnings leap
From cloud to cloud in majesty.

* Light House.

At length, a flash from distant gun
  Is followed by a rocket's glare,
Which rises like the morning sun,
  And bursts, in globes of fire, in air.

"*A Blockade-Runner off the bar!*"
  The rocket signals to the fleet;
"Fort Caswell" answers from afar,
  With storm of iron hail and sleet.

Our fleet steams up in triple line,
  To close upon the "Runner" brave,
Now pressing on with bold design,
  To pass or sink beneath the wave.

Thick darkness reigns on sea and shore,
  Save when the lightning 'lumes the air,
Or "Caswell's" guns of largest bore
  An instant flash with lurid glare.

As o'er the deep we swiftly fly,
  The ocean foam our only trail,
A voice sings out from mainmast high,
  "A sail, off starboard beam, *strange sail!*"

Amid the clouds now moving free,
  The lightnings for an instant blaze,
And as the gleam illumes the sea,
  Reveals the "Runner" to our gaze.

The guns upon our upper deck
  Pour out their thunder on the air!—
We look to see a helpless wreck,
  And *lo! no sign of sail is there!*

In arms of black squall swiftly borne,
The "Blockade-Runner" flies away;
"Oh, for an hour of smiling morn!"
"Oh, for a glance of shining day!"

The prize is fled, escaped to sea,
And there remains but this to say—
That "Blockade-chasing" seems to me
Like hunting pins 'mong stacks of hay!

The Waters and Country around New Orleans, p. 205.

CHAPTER XV.

The Preparation to attack New Orleans—General Butler—Farragut—Progress of the Enterprise—Forts Philip and Jackson—Fire Rafts—The Signal Shell —The Bombardment opens.

SHIP Island, a sea-girdled sand-bar about eight miles in length and less than a mile in width, lying on the coast near New Orleans, was made the rendezvous of the forces which were to move against New Orleans. The forts guarding it were of course the first object, for when the defences of a city are gone, it generally fails without further struggle into the hands of the victors. And you know our Government had declared its purpose to recapture the fortresses of the United States, and unfurl once more the Stars and Stripes over them.

On this desolate spot the rebels had erected fortifications. The first thing to be done was to *get* the island. So the Government sent the good steamer Massachusetts with a company of marines to clear the sandbank of traitors, and kindle anew the light-house lamp, whose flame had been the mariner's guide before treason put it out, in the attempt to extinguish the hope of the world by the overthrow of the republic.

General Phelps, commanding the Ninth Connecticut and Twenty-sixth Massachusetts, landed on the island early in the winter. The number of troops was soon increased to several thousands. With the advent of spring, Major-General Butler reached Ship Island, to the joy of the "boys," weary of the inactivity on their desert-like Juan Fernandez.

During the few succeeding weeks, occasionally a shot was exchanged between the passing rebel steamers and ours protecting the harbor, and expeditions were sent over to the main land, routing the enemy there.

Commodore D. D. Porter's mortar fleet of twenty vessels and eight steamers towing the ammunition schooners, arrived from Key West. Commodore Porter is a son worthy of his sire, of Farragut's old friend and captain.

April 15th the fleet hoisted sail again, and soon after joined the blockading squadron and other war-steamers from the east, riding in the Mississippi. The entire armada was under the command of Commodore Farragut, whose flag-ship was the Hartford. Pilot Town, four miles from the Gulf, was taken, and the mortar flotilla anchored near it.

The formidable defences of the southern metropolis were Forts Jackson and St. Phillip, sixty miles below it, two magnificent fortresses, whose scientific and elaborate construction defied attack; and the garrisons within them, with the Confederacy around them, laughed the united fleets to scorn. They were reared by our own Government to guard from foreign invasion the common purchase of Revolutionary blood. They stand at a sharp bend of the "Father of Waters," and before them the current is rapid.

Fort Jackson, on the west bank, was a pentagonal fortress, presenting two of its massive brick walls to the river, and three facing the land. On the former are sixteen casemated guns, and on the other sides twenty-four pound howitzers, covering with their fire the ditches. A drawbridge, ten feet in width, connects it with the mainland approach. Three-quarters of a mile distant is Fort St. Phillip, on the opposite shore, and above Jackson. The tremendous armament numbered one hundred and eighty pieces of different calibre. In addition to these, an iron cable was stretched across the river, resting on seven old hulks anchored in the current, and guarded by a well-manned gunboat. Still higher up the stream were eighteen iron-clads, steam rams, and floating batteries. Fire-rafts were also ready to be ignited and sent among an invading fleet. It is not strange that the fifteen hundred men who garrisoned the forts felt secure, and awaited scornfully the Yankee naval force.

Hear the reply of the gallant Farragut, when officers

of English and French war-ships expressed the belief, which a Union man in New Orleans had previously written in his correspondence with the North, "No fleet can pass up the river without a miraculous interposition:" "You may be right. But I was sent here to make the attempt. I came here to reduce or pass the forts, and to take New Orleans, and *I shall try it.*"

The preparation to move toward the city went on in the fleet. Sails were taken down, loose rigging made fast to the masts, decks cleared, and armor of heavy chain cables stretched along the sides of the wooden ships.

He called a council of war, and listened patiently to the views of his officers, which were not harmonious upon the daring enterprise. The decision of the commanding mind is a clear scintillation of its hitherto unerring light, embodied in a general order: "The flag-officer having heard all the opinions expressed by the different commanders, is of the opinion, *that whatever is to be done, will have to be done quickly.* When, in the opinion of the flag-officer, the propitious time has arrived, the signal will be made to weigh and advance to the conflict. He will make a signal for close action, *and abide the result—conquer or be conquered.*"

Of these men-of-war, thus stripped for combat, says a beholder: "They have an air of strength and massiveness, which is simply terrible."

To deceive the enemy, the vessels were daubed with

the mud of the river banks, rendering them almost undistinguishable in the distance from the river, colored with the same material, or from the shores. Commodore Porter, son of Farragut's old friend, contributed largely, by his forethought and skill, to the perfection of the arrangements. Thus the two "middies," many years before, were not only working together, but were worthy of their sire and commander. It was now the middle of April, 1862.

Six gunboats, with their masts enwreathed with foliage, to resemble the forest between them and the forts, which concealed the hulls, drift along in close procession. Nearing the enemy, the crews added the disguise of marsh reeds and other vegetation, fastened to the vessels' sides. The Hartford, Pensacola, Richmond, Brooklyn, and Mississippi, followed the mortars.

On the 15th, a sudden alarm was signalled through the fleet. Look up the swift current, and see that fiercely burning bonfire sweeping right down upon it. A raft with its cords of pine in a blaze, is running with the glow of wrath upon the Union armada. Providentially, before reaching its goal it grounded and burned to the water's edge. Commodore Porter made prompt provision for a similar assault. One hundred and fifty boats were furnished with picked crews, axes, grapnel ropes, and buckets, to intercept the flaming heralds of treason.

The night came down with neither moon nor stars

visible. All was still and curtained with gloom, through which ship-lights glimmered, and anxious eyes were peering for signs of danger. The grim war-ships lay quietly, only as their hearts of iron throbbed with fiery impatience for the coming conflict. A gleam of fire! Then the signal rockets streamed through the night. A little nearer, and the fire-raft was discovered again rushing down the tide. The hundred and fifty boats were soon moving like spectres through the darkness. A few gunboats also left their moorings. Over all was shed the lurid light of the floating fire, reddening the shores with its fearful torch of civil strife. The gunboats passed the hissing raft, the smaller boats darted around it to secure it and drag it away from the fleet. Such a scene is rarely beheld even in time of war. Words of command, blows of the axes, the hammer driving home the fastening, echoed in the weird light of the strange wild scene. Then away the fire-pile moved, and in a few moments *expires.* Silence was restored, and nature reposed under the wings of darkness.

The 16th brought the defiant challenge from Fort Jackson, in the form of a shell falling among the Union fleet. The mortar-boats replied with a terrific bombardment—each of their three divisions firing two hours in succession, then pausing to cool. Thus passed the first day's conflict, sending its ominous echoes away to the doomed city. A week passed, and yet no substantial progress had been made in reducing the forts. The admiral formed the bold design of moving by the gigantic guardians of the Mississippi, through chains, floating batteries, and rams.

At midnight of 21st, Lieutenant Commander Crosby, of the Pinola, Lieutenant Commander Caldwell, of the Itasca, stole up the stream to the chain, right under the guns which could have soon destroyed them if they were discovered, and broke it. Just at this crisis was displayed the comprehensive and executive genius of the admiral. When the chain was cut, and the boats supporting it sagged asunder—prevented from swinging by the anchors to which each rode—there was left in the centre a gap or passage-way like the opening of a drawbridge. Thereupon the rebels built, lit, and maintained large fires on either side of the river, so that when Farragut should attempt to pass by night, their blaze would not only render his movements visible to every battery, but enable the forts to bring a complete cross-fire to bear upon him. Some of the admiral's officers suggested that nothing would be easier than to send a few boat-crews ashore and extinguish the fires. "No! no! by no means," said the commander, "those fires are the light-houses by which I mean to steam through the gap in the chain, throw a few shells or shot at them, to give the rebels an idea that we want them to put them out, and thus incite them to more strenuous exertions to keep them bright and alive." The result proved the wisdom of the admiral's instant decision of mind.

CHAPTER XVI.

The Advance—The Terrible Conflict—The Fire-raft and Rams—Victory—Thanksgiving—Anecdotes of the Admiral—The Effect of the Victory on the Nation—Up the River—Passing Port Hudson—The Second Gauntlet of Fire.

AS the signal arose at two o'clock on the morning of the 24th, which was two red lights, too common to attract the attention of the enemy, Commodore Farragut's fleet started on its voyage of victory or ruin. The advance was made in two columns. In the van were the three magnificent ships, the Hartford, the Brooklyn, and the Richmond, followed by the gunboats Sciota, Iroquois, Kennebec, Pinola, Itasca, and Winona; the second column by the Pensacola and the Mississippi. They all made for the chasm in the barrier of hulks and chains, keeping up an incessant fire upon the forts, and, as one after another they passed through, the vessels of the first division ranged themselves to assail Fort St. Philip, and the second Fort Jackson, while all alike were prepared to attack and repel the rebel rams and gunboats, as occasion might require. "It may be safely said that such a naval conflict was never winessed on this earth before. The enemy were on the alert, and the beacon-fires soon blazed so brightly as to expose every movement of the fleet; and the whole stormy scene was illumined with a lurid glare, which added vastly to its sublimity, and its almost fiendlike horror. The Cayuga was the first which passed the chain-boom, under a terrible fire from both of the forts, which struck her repeatedly from stem to stern. The rest of the sqnadron rapidly followed. They were now directly abreast of the forts, exposed to the direct action of their guns, while the river above was crowded with the fire-rafts, rams, and gunboats of the foe.

"They all came plunging down together upon the heroic fleet. First came an immense fire-raft, pushed by the ram Manassas, directly upon the flag-ship Hartford. In endeavoring to avoid it, the ship was crowded ashore, and the flaming raft was pushed down upon its side. In a moment the majestic ship seemed enveloped in flames, halfway up to her tops. Fortunately the ship was backed off from the shoal, and by immense exertions of the fire department the flames were extinguished. The thunder of over three hundred guns from the forts, the rebel gunboats, and the national fleet, joined with the distant booming of the mortars, filled the air with a continuous roar, louder than heaven's heaviest thunders.

"Red-hot shot and bursting shell were falling with frightful execution on ship and battlement. The whole scene was soon so enveloped in the sulphurous smoke of the battle, that friends could with difficulty be distinguished from foes, and often the flash of opposing guns alone guided the fire. The rebels fought with that desperation which was to be expected of Americans, even when engaged in an infamous cause. While the national ships were yet under the fire of the forts, they were assailed by the monster rams and floating batteries which the foe held in reserve. These enormous rams, aided by the swift current, and under full headway of steam, dashed with their iron prows upon our ships, discharging at close range their heavy guns as reckless as if no harm could touch them. It is impossible to recount the exploits of the gallant men who fought beneath the stars and stripes, in these hours of deadly encounter.

"Every ship in the fleet signalized itself by heroism which could not be surpassed. We cannot record the deeds of all; let us allude to a few as specimens of the rest. The United States steamship Brooklyn, in the darkness, and while exposed to the hottest fire, became entangled in the barricading hulks and chains. In attempting to extricate the ship her bow grazed the shore. She, however, worked her way through, when the ram Manassas came rushing upon her from the gloom. At the distance of ten feet the ram discharged her shot, which pierced the ship, and then, with a crash, struck her side, battering in the starboard gangway. The chain armor saved the ship from destruction, and the ram slid off and disappeared in the darkness.

"Fort Jackson, in the liftings of the smoke, caught a glimpse of the majestic ship, and opened upon her a raking fire. Just then a large rebel steamer came rushing up on the port broadside. When at the distance of but sixty yards, the Brooklyn poured into the audacious stranger one single volley of shell and red-hot shot, and the fragments of the steamer, in a mass of crackling flame, drifted down the stream.

"The Brooklyn, still groping its way along, lighted by the flames of an approaching fire-raft, and yet enveloped in its resinous smoke, soon found itself abreast of St. Philip, almost touching the shore. The ship chanced to be in such a position that she could bring almost every gun to bear. Tarrying for a moment, she poured into the fort such a storm of grape and canister as completely to silence the work. The men stationed in the tops of the frigate said that, by the light of their bursting shrapnels, they could see the garrison 'running like sheep for more comfortable quarters.'

"The Brooklyn then rushed into the nest of rebel gunboats, fighting them indiscriminately, with her broadsides striking the most terrific blows, and continuing the contest, in connection with the other vessels, for an hour and a half, until the rebel fleet was annihilated. After the action was over, Commodore Farragut took the hand of Capt. Craven, of the Brooklyn, in both of his, and said: 'You and your noble ship have been the salvation of my squadron. You were in a complete blaze of fire; so much so that I supposed your ship was burning up. I never saw such rapid and precise firing. It never was surpassed, and probably never was equalled.'

"The Mississippi encountered the ram Manassas, rushing upon her at full speed. The noble old frigate, undaunted, instead of evading the blow, turned to meet her antagonist, and, with all steam on, made a plunge at the monster. Just as the blow was to come which would decide whose head was to be broken open, the Manassas, taking counsel of discretion, dodged. But as she glided by, a point-blank broadside from the immense armament of the Mississippi, swept off her smoke-stack, crashed through her iron sides, and set her on fire. The crew took to the shore, and the redoubtable ram drifted, a total wreck, down the stream. The nondescript monster presented a curious spectacle, as she floated along, the flames bursting through the broken chinks of her mail, her shot-fractures, and her port-holes. Commodore Porter wishing to save her as a curiosity, sent some boats to pass a hawser around the ram and secure it to the shore. Scarcely was this done when the monster uttered, as it were, an expiring groan, as the water rushed in, driving the air and the belching flames through her bow-port, and then, 'like a huge animal, she gave a plunge and disappeared under the water.' The achievements of the Varuna, under Captain Boggs, were among the crowning glories of this eventful day. It has been well said, he 'fought a battle fully equal in desperate hardihood and resolute bravery to the famous sea-fight of John Paul Jones, which nothing human could surpass.' After taking or destroying six of the enemy's vessels, an unarmored point was pierced, and while the water rushed in, the crew jumped into the boats of the Oneida, sent for their rescue, as she went down with her dead, 'victorious in death,' her flag still flying, covered with glory."

The next morning dawned on drifting wrecks and smoke, through and beyond which the Union fleet was marching for New Orleans. A despatch was sent to General Butler that the way was clear for landing his troops. Soon after, at noon, the *armada*, having had only three gunboats disabled, thirty men killed, and one hundred and ten wounded, moored in front of the city.

The pride of the boastful chivalry, already humbled on the 26th, was fallen, and in the dust, under the national colors floating from the public buildings.

After the victory was complete, he issued an order for the observance of "thanksgiving to Almighty God" for the success. He did not blush to acknowledge his dependence upon Him before whom even "the nations are as grasshoppers"—an illustrious example of a warrior commending the Gospel of Peace.

He can be stern and severe when duty requires it. As he was standing on the quarter-deck of the flag-ship of New Orleans, a gunboat started out from the dock, and not making allowance for the current, ran directly into the bows of the flag-ship, doing considerable injury. "Who commands that vessel?" asked the indignant Admiral. On being informed, he said, "Send that child home. Send that child home." In a few moments another officer was sent on board to take command.

Among the anecdotes that disclose his kindness, and patient attention to the wants of those under his command, is a pleasant incident that occurred about this time. At one time, as he was going on board one of the vessels at New Orleans, all the firemen met him at the gangway, and asked if a wind-sail might be put down into the fire-room to give them more air. "Certainly," said the admiral, "you should have had one before." He then ordered the captain of the ship to give them the largest wind-sail that could be made—and it was done.

Then followed the landing of the troops of General Butler near Fort St. Philip; the surrender of the fortress; the terrific explosion of the rebel battery, the Louisiana; and the triumphant administration of the *civil* hero of

New Orleans—the commander of the land forces in the conquest.

In every view the victory was a grand success for the Union cause. Six forts, eighteen gunboats, and twelve hundred prisoners were taken. The proudest rebel city was captured, and all rebeldom groaned over the loss, while affecting indifference as to the ultimate result upon the contest. The tidings, "New Orleans is taken!" flew over the land on lightning-wing, causing the wildest enthusiasm.

Congress passed a vote of thanks to the hero of the great victory, and the President added his own warm congratulations. With New Orleans safely under the Stars and Stripes, Flag-Officer Farragut pushed up the "Father of Waters." On the 27th he reached and passed the batteries above the city without injury.

The object of the expedition was to communicate with Flag-Officer Davis, commanding the Mississippi squadron, look after the rebel ram Arkansas, and complete arrangements for a joint attack on Vicksburg. A bombardment proved fruitless, because the high banks, bristling with ordnance, could not be battered down, nor the fortress taken by shot from the decks of the fleet, without the co-operation of land forces. Eighteen days later, Farragut returned, successfully repassed the batteries, and made Pensacola the place of rendezvous for the squadron. Meanwhile Congress had made a law creating the rank of rear-admiral, and conferred on him, July 11th, its earliest honors, for his brilliant conduct at New Orleans.

Texas now became the field mainly of the admiral's operations. An expedition was ordered in the autumn against Corpus Christi, followed by others against Sabine Pass and Galveston, all of which were successful in capturing the important points. Several months were occupied in similar operations. The guerrillas and rebel towns on the coast, and blockade-runners for Mobile and Galveston, all received his unwearied attention. With the advent of the spring of 1863, a larger theatre for the lion of naval warfare opened.

General Sherman's expedition against Vicksburg in the winter had failed, because the cowardly surrender of Holly Springs deranged the magnificent plans of General Grant in connection with him, and another attempt was to be made.

General Grant had determined to get in the rear of Vicksburg, and wanted Admiral Farragut to sail above Port Hudson, while Admiral Foote went below Vicksburg, uniting in the reduction of batteries there, to clear the way for Grant, whose troops were to advance down the west side of the river; and otherwise to aid the bold enterprise as he might have opportunity. Admiral Farragut at once led with his flag-ship, the Hartford, followed by the Richmond, the Mississippi, the Monongahela, with the gunboats Kineo, Albatross, and Genesee, and six mortar-boats; the latter were to assist in the bombardment, but remain below the batteries.

The fleet moved toward Port Hudson near the middle of March. On the 14th just after noon, the mortars opened their fire on the fortifications, second to none in strength but those at Vicksburg, on the Mississippi. A detachment of troops was also sent in the rear, to confuse the garrisons, while the admiral got ready for his *night-work.* Then occurred one of those grand and unusual exhibitions of naval warfare, of which the passage of Forts Jackson and St. Philip was unrivalled in terrible sublimity. The evening was dark, but Confederate scouts had watched the Union fleet, and given notice of preparation for some movement to the garrison.

Immediately a tremendous bonfire was kindled on the heights, and poured its flood of lurid light down the cannon-bordered bluffs upon the waters just where the ships would pass the most formidable works. In the reflected flames, each vessel and its motions would be distinctly visible as in the light of day. It was a crisis to try the metal not only of ordnance, but of the Admiral's character. He had never quailed in the moment of peril, and now was calmer than ever. Right onward toward the flashing surface over which frowned the heaviest rebel cannon, his squadron advanced.

A description of what followed, already written, I laid

aside, my young reader, to give you instead extracts from a letter penned on board the Richmond, a most graphic, vivid picture of the naval action. You find the good name *Essex* again:

"We had left the mortar-boats well astern, when a sulphurous light was seen gleaming on the shore, on our port side. Flashing up for a moment, a dull explosion followed. It was evidently an imperfect rocket. Another was essayed; but, instead of ascending, it ran along the surface of the river close to the bank. A little further up a third was tried, and with complete success. It ascended high in the air, where it burst in the usual manner. Instantaneously it was answered by a field-piece from the opposite shore, aimed at the Hartford. The Admiral was not slow in returning the compliment. Three or four guns fired from the flag-ship in rapid succession testified to the alacrity with which the wager of battle was accepted.

"The return of the rebel fire by the Hartford, was promptly followed up by a hot fire from the artillery pieces of the rebels, and quite a brisk action ensued between them. The scene, as viewed from the Richmond, was both brilliant and spirited. The flashes of the guns, both on shore and afloat, were incessant, while the roar of cannon kept up a deafening and almost incessant sound. Great judgment was here necessary to prevent the Richmond from running into the Hartford, and, in fact, to keep the war-vessels generally from running into each other.

"And now was heard a thundering roar, equal in volume to a whole park of artillery. This was followed by a rushing sound, accompanied by a howling noise that beggars description. Again and again was the sound repeated, till the vast expanse of heaven rang with the awful minstrelsy. It was apparent that the mortar-boats had opened fire. Of this I was soon convinced on casting my eyes aloft. Never shall I forget the sight that then met my astonished vision. Shooting upward at an angle of forty-five degrees, with the rapidity of lightning, small globes of golden flame were seen sailing through the pure ether—not a steady, unfading flame, but corruscating like the fitful gleam of a fire-fly—now visible and anon invisible. Like a flying star of the sixth magnitude, the terrible missile—a thirteen-inch shell—nears its zenith, up and still up—higher and higher. Its flight now becomes much slower, till on reaching its utmost altitude, its centrifugal force becomes counteracted by the earth's attraction, it describes a parabolic curve, and down, down it comes, bursting, it may be, ere it reaches *terra firma*, but probably alighting in the rebel works ere it explodes, where it scatters death and destruction around. But while the mortar-boats were at work, the Essex was not idle. Unmanageable as she is, especially in so strong a current, she did not follow the rest of the fleet, but remained at the head of the 'bummers,' doing admirable service with her heavy guns.

"All this time the Richmond had to hang back, as Admiral Farragut seemed to be so enamored with the sport in which he was engaged as to be in no hurry to pass by. Once or twice, in consequence of the dense column of smoke that now rolled over the river, our bowsprit was almost over the taffrail of the Hartford, and there was an incessant call on the part of Second Lieutenant Terry, who commanded the forward part of the ship, to stop the engines. And here I may as well say that this gallant young officer behaved in the most chivalrous manner throughout the entire engagement, cheering on the men, and encouraging them, by his example, to stand to their guns like men, though little of this they required to induce them to perform their whole duty.

"The Richmond had by this time got within range of the rebel field-batteries, which opened fire on her. I had all along thought that we would open fire from our bow-guns, on the top-gallant forecastle, and that, after discharging a few broadsides from the starboard side, the action would be wound up by a parting compliment from our stern-chasers. To my surprise, however, we opened at once from our broadside guns. The effect was startling, as the sound was unexpected; but beyond this I really experienced no inconvenience from the concussion. There was nothing unpleasant to the ear, and the jar to the ship was really quite unappreciable. It may interest the uninitiated to be informed how a broadside is fired from a vessel-of-war. I was told on board the Richmond that all the guns were sometimes fired off simultaneously, though it is not a very usual course, as it strains the ship. Last night the broadsides were fired by commencing at the forward gun, and firing all the rest off in rapid succession, as fast almost as the ticking of a watch. The effect was grand and terrific; and, if the guns were rightly pointed—a difficult thing in the dark, by the way—they could not fail in carrying death and destruction among the enemy.

"Of course we did not have every thing our own way, for the enemy poured in his shot and shell as thick as hail. Over, ahead, astern, all around us flew the death-dealing missiles, the hissing, screaming, whistling, shrieking, and howling of which rivalled Pandemonium. It must not be supposed, however, that because our broadside-guns were the tools we principally worked, that our bow and stern-chasers were idle. We soon opened with our bow eighty-pounder Dahlgren, which was followed up not long after by the guns astern, giving evidence to the fact that we had passed some of the batteries.

"While seated on the 'fish-davit,' on the top-gallant forecastle—the Hartford and the Richmond blazing away at the time—a most fearful wail arose from the river, first on our port-bow then on the beam. A man was evidently overboard, probably from the Hartford or the Genesee, then just ahead. The cry was: 'Help, oh! help!' 'Help, oh! help!' 'Man overboard,' called out Lieutenant Terry; 'throw him a rope.' But, poor fellow, who could assist him in such a strait? We were in action; every man was at his gun; to lower a boat would be folly; in fact, it could not be done with any hope of success. Consequently, although the man was evidently a good swimmer, to judge by his unfailing cries for help for a long time, nothing could be done to rescue him, and he floated astern of us, still sending up that wailing cry for help, but without effect. The terrible current of the Mississippi was too much for him, and he, without doubt, sank beneath the waves of the mighty river.

"Just after this fearful incident firing was heard astern of us, and it was soon ascertained that the Monongahela, with her consort, the Kineo, and the Mississippi were in action. The Monongahela carries a couple of two hundred-pounder rifled Parrott guns, besides other ticklers. At first I credited the roar of her amiable two hundred-pounders to the 'bummers,' till I was undeceived, when I recalled my experience in front of Yorktown last spring, and the opening of fire from similar guns from Wormley's Creek. All I can say is, the noise was splendid. The action now became general. The roar of cannon was incessant, and the flashes from the guns, together with with the flight of the shells from the mortar-boats, made up a combination of sound and sight impossible to describe.

To add to the horrors of the night, while it contributed toward the enhancement of a certain terrible beauty, dense clouds of smoke began to envelop the river, shutting out from view the several vessels, and confounding them with the batteries. It was very difficult to know how to steer to prevent running ashore, perhaps right under a rebel battery, or into a consort. Upward and upward rolled the smoke, shutting out of view the beautiful stars and obscuring the vision on every side. Then it was that the order was passed: 'Boys, don't fire till you see the flash from the enemy's guns.' That was our only guide through the 'palpable obscurity.'

"But this sole dependence on the flashes was likely to be attended with serious consequence, as the following incident will show:

"We had got nearly into the middle of the hornet's nest, when an officer on the top-gallant forecastle called out: 'Ready with the port-gun.' The gun was got ready and pointed, and was about to be discharged, when Lieutenant Perry called out: 'Hold on; you are about to fire into the Hartford.' And such was the fact; for the flash of the Hartford's guns at that moment revealed the spars and rigging of that vessel. Consequently the gun was not fired, nor was it discharged during the engagement, the fighting being confined entirely to the starboard side.

"Still the fight went on, and still the roar of cannon and the screaming, howling, whistling of shot and shell continued to make 'night hideous.' Still, too, the pure atmosphere was befouled with the smell of 'villanous saltpetre' and obscured with smoke, through the opaque mass of which the stars refused to twinkle. Intermingled with the boom of the cannonade arose the cries of the wounded and the shouts of their friends, suggesting that they should be taken below for treatment. So thick was the smoke that we had to cease firing several times; and to add to the horrors of the night it was next to impossible to tell whether we were running into the Hartford or going ashore, and, if the latter, on which bank, or whether some of the other vessels were about to run into us or into each other. All this time the fire was kept up on both sides incessantly. It seems, however, that we succeeded in silencing the lower batteries of field-pieces. The men must have been driven from their guns; and no wonder if they were, in that terrific storm of iron.

"While a brisk fire was kept up from the decks of the several vessels, the howitzers in the tops were not permitted to remain idle. Intermingled with the more sullen roar of the larger guns, the sharp, short crack of the brass pieces was heard from their elevated positions, adding harmony to the melody of the terrific concert.

"The phrase is familiar to most persons who have read accounts of sea-fights that took place about fifty years ago; but it is difficult for the uninitiated to realize all the horrors conveyed in 'muzzle to muzzle.' For the first time I had, last night, an opportunity of knowing what the phrase really meant. Let the reader consult the map, and it will be seen that the central battery is situated about the middle of the segment of a circle I have already compared to a horse-shoe in shape, though it may be better understood by the term 'crescent.' This battery stands on a bluff so high that a vessel in passing immediately underneath cannot elevate her guns sufficiently to reach those on the battery; neither can the guns on the battery be sufficiently depressed to bear on the passing ship. In this position the rebel batteries on the two horns of the crescent can enfilade the passing vessel, pouring in a terrible cross-fire, which the vessel can return, though at a great disadvantage, from her bow and stern-chasers.

"We fully realized this last night; for, as we got within short-range, the enemy poured into us a terrible fire of grape and canister, which we were not slow to return—our guns being double-shotted, each with a stand of both grape and canister. Every vessel in its turn was exposed to the same fiery ordeal on nearing the centre battery, and right promptly did their gallant tars return the compliment. This was the hottest part of the engagement. We were literally muzzle to muzzle, the distance between us and the enemy's guns being not more than twenty yards, though to me it seemed to be only as many feet. In fact, the battle of Port Hudson has been pronounced by officers and seamen who were engaged in it, and who were present at the passage of Fort St. Philip and Fort Jackson, below New Orleans, and had participated in the fights of Fort Donelson, Fort Henry, Island Number Ten, Vicksburg, etc., as the severest in the naval history of the present war.

"Shortly after this close engagemement we seemed to have passed the worst. The enemy's shot and shell no longer swept our decks like a hail-storm; but the fire from the batteries was kept up in a desultory manner. The starboard bow-gun could no longer be brought to bear. Consequently Lieutenant Terry ordered the men on the top-gallant forecastle to leave the guns in that part of the ship, and to descend to the main deck to help work the broadside guns. Our stern-chasers, of course, were still available, for the purpose of giving the enemy a parting blessing. I left my station on the top-gallant forecastle shortly after the men who had been working the bow-guns, and passed under where I had been sitting, taking up my station on the port side, just opposite the forward gun on the starboard side, where but a few minutes before a shell had exploded.

"I was not long in this position when there came a blinding flash through the very port I was opposite to, revealing a high bank right opposite, so close that a biscuit might have been tossed from the summit on board the Richmond. Simultaneously there came a loud roar, and I thought the shot had passed through the port I was opposite to. Indeed, so close were we to the battery that the flash, the report, and the arrival of the shot, crashing and tearing through our bulwarks, were instantaneous, there not being the intermission of a second between.

"It must have been about this time that Lieutenant Commander Cummings, the executive officer of the Richmond, was standing on the bridge that connects the starboard with the port gangway, with his speaking-trumpet in his hand, cheering the men. Near him stood Captain Alden, when a conical shot of large calibre passed through the hammocks, over the starboard gangway, taking off the left leg of the lieutenant just above the ankle, battering his speaking-trumpet (a prize) flat, and knocking Captain Alden down with the windage, and went through the smoke-stack. Mr. Cummings was immediately taken below, where his wound was promptly attended to by Dr. Henderson, the ship's surgeon, but not before the brave young man had lost a large quantity of blood on his way down. On being carried below he used the following patriotic words, which are worthy of becoming historical: 'I would willingly give my other leg so that we could but pass the batteries.'

"The Rev. Dr. Bacon, the loyal rector of Christ Church, New Orleans, who was acting as chaplain on board the Richmond, was on the bridge when Mr. Cummings received his terrible wound. He fortunately escaped unhurt, though he had been all over the ship, in the thickest of the fight, carrying messages and exhorting and encouraging the men.

"It was no easy matter, in the midst of such a dense cloud of smoke, to know where to point our guns. Even the flashes of the enemy's guns shone dimly through the thick gloom. Several times the order was given to cease fire, so as to allow the smoke to clear away; but, as there was scarcely a breath of wind stirring, this was a very slow process; still the order was necessary, to prevent the several vessels from running into each other. In this respect the rebels had a decided advantage over us; for while they did not stand in danger of collision, neither was there any apprehension of firing into their friends. The wide river was before them, and if they did not hit our vessels at each discharge, they could but miss at the worst.

"Matters had gone on this way for nearly an hour and a half—the first gun having been fired at about half-past eleven o'clock—when, to my astonishment, I heard some shells whistling over our port side. Did the rebels have batteries on the right bank of the river? was the query that naturally suggested itself to me. To this the response was given that we had turned back. I soon discovered that it was too true. Our return was, of course, more rapid than our passage up. The rebels did not molest us much, and I do not believe one of their shots took effect while we were running down rapidly with the current.

"We were soon quietly at anchor, and were busy discussing the events of the fight, exchanging congratulations and comparing notes, when the lookout man in the maintop hailed the deck as follows:

"'On deck there!'

"'Hallo!'

"'A large fire ahead!'

"'Where away?'

"'Just above the bend.'

"'What is it like?'

"'Like a fire-raft.'

"On this Captain Alden, to whom the circumstance was duly reported by the officers of the deck, sings out:

"'Keep a good lookout. Man the bow guns, and stand by to slip the cable.'

"Shortly after this a small steamer came down, the master of which informed Captain Alden that the Mississippi was on fire.

"In the dense smoke that prevailed, excluding every object from view, the glorious old Mississippi went ashore right opposite the centre and worst battery. She was soon discovered by the enemy. Up to this time she had not sustained any serious injury. She now became a standing target for the whole range of rebel batteries. The rebels began to pour into her a perfect shower of shot and shell, which was promptly returned by the Mississippi. This murderous work continued for half an hour.

Finding it impossible to escape, Capt. Smith judiciously but reluctantly gave orders to set the ship on fire to prevent her falling into the hands of the rebels. Accordingly her after-part was fired, the rebels all the time continuing to pour in their shot and shell as fast as they could bring their guns to bear. During this part of the contest no fewer than two hundred and fifty rounds were fired from the Mississippi. The artillery practice of the rebels would have been worthy of a better cause. The Mississippi was riddled through and through. Four men were known to have been killed ere the ship was abandoned. Among them was Acting Master Kelly, the whole of whose abdomen was shot away. Three were ascertained to have been wounded. There may have been some more casualties, but it is impossible to tell to what extent at present, though a great many exaggerated stories are afloat on the subject. Several were known to have jumped overboard soon after the ship was set on fire, and there can be no doubt that some of them were drowned.

"Soon after the vessel had been fired two shells came crashing through her, exploding and setting fire to some turpentine and oil which they upset. This caused the flames to spread, whereupon a master's mate hurried on to the gundeck and reported that the flames had reached the entrance to the magazine. The ship was then at once abandoned, and all hands on board, including the wounded men, were put on shore on the bank of the river opposite Port Hudson. This was accompanied by a deafening yell of exultation from the rebels on perceiving the blazing up of the fire. The Mississippi burned till she became lightened, to which the removal of nearly three hundred men contributed, when she swung off into deep water. She had grounded with her head up stream; but on swinging off she turned completely round, presenting her head down the river, which position she retained till she blew up.

"At length it was reported on board the Richmond that the Mississippi was coming down, and we all turned out on the poop-deck to see the sight. It was a most magnificent spectacle. From the midships to the stern the noble vessel was enveloped in a sheet of flame, while fire-wreaths ran up the shrouds, played around the mainmast, twisted and writhed like fiery serpents. Onward she came, keeping near to the right bank, still bow foremost, as regularly as if she was steered by a pilot. It was, indeed, a wonderful sight. Captain Smith, her recent commander, and several of her officers, who had by this time arrived on board the Richmond, assembled on the poop-deck, their emotion almost too great for words. Next to his wife, children, or sweetheart, there is nothing that a sailor loves more than his ship—nothing that he regrets the loss of so much; and, in the absence of the above-mentioned domestic, ties, his ship is to him wife, child, and sweetheart. The feeling of regret at the loss of his ship is enhanced when, as in the case of the Mississippi, the gallant craft has achieved historical renown. No wonder, then, that the officers of the Mississippi should feel a sinking at the heart on witnessing the destruction of their floating home, while they were powerless to save her.

"As she arrived opposite the port side of the Richmond, some apprehension was entertained that her port broadsides might give us a parting salute of not a very agreeable nature. Captain Smith assured Captain Alden, however, that her port guns had all been discharged. Just as she had cleared us, her starboard guns began to go off. This was accompanied by the explosion of the shells she had on deck, ready for use. These exploded at short intervals. The flames now began to increase in volume from amidships to the stern, and the howitzer on the maintop was discharged with the heat. Majestically the gallant craft—gallant even in its last moments—moved down the stream, till, turning the bend at the lower part of Prophet Island, she was hidden from our view, and nothing more was seen but a white glare, shooting up skyward. Shell after shell still exploded at intervals, and thus a couple of hours passed away till the Mississippi was some eight or ten miles below the Richmond. The shells now begin to explode more rapidly, indicating that the fire has reached the shell-room, and cannot be far from the powder magazine. This proves to be the fact; for presently a sudden glare of bright flame shoots upward toward the zenith, spreading skyward, in the form of an inverted cone; an interval of a few seconds elapses; then comes a stunning roar, causing the Richmond to tremble from truck to keelson, and the gallant Mississippi, that so long 'has braved the battle and the breeze,' is no more; all that remains of her is sunk in the bosom of the mighty river from which she derived her name.

"Passing through the starboard side of the Richmond, amidships, a conical eighty-pounder passed through a pile of cordage on the berth-deck, narrowly missing some powder-boys who were handing up ammunition. Thence it entered the machinery-room, passing through and smashing the steam-drum, and damaging both safety-valves, so as to prevent them from closing. Taking its course under the steam-chest, the shot came out on the other side, when it broke in two, and both pieces dropped below. Here I may take this opportunity of mentioning that Confederate iron, in these regions, is a very inferior metal. It is not half smelted, but right in the centre are large stones.

"Early this morning the decks of the Richmond presented a melancholy spectacle. Where the two men fell there was a great pool of clotted gore, which I saw a seaman tossing overboard with a shovel. The whitewashed decks, too, were any thing but tidy; but, hey! presto! as if by magic, the stalwart arms of some two or three hundred men, with the aid of a plentiful supply of Mississippi water, have made every thing as clean and neat as a lady's boudoir. The bodies of the two men who were killed have been removed forward, and to them has been added the body of the boatswain's mate, who lost both legs and an arm, and who has since died. The three bodies have been neatly sewed up in their hammocks, and they are to be put into coffins for interment on shore. Headboards, with their names inscribed on them, will be placed at the heads of their graves, so that the bodies may be reclaimed at any time by their friends or relatives."

Soon after occurred one of those daring adventures, many of which are unrecorded, related in a letter from New Orleans at that time. The Admiral wanted despatches, and the Yankee boys determined to get them beyond Port Hudson, as you will see:

"New Orleans, *April* 18.

"Much interest is felt in the fortunes of Admiral Farragut by every loyal man in the country, and his assured safety is a source of congratulation among good men everywhere.

"On Tuesday morning, April 14th, Lieutenants H. B. Skinner and C. C. Dean of General Dudley's staff, and Lieutenant Tenney, Quartermaster of the Thirtieth

Massachusetts volunteers, went up from Baton Rouge to Port Hamilton in the Richmond, they having volunteered to go across the point opposite Port Hudson, and carry despatches from below to the Admiral, who was to be at the mouth of False River on Wednesday morning. Captain Roe and Lieutenant Herbert of the signal corps accompanied the expedition. During the sail up an additional mast was put above the main topmast of the Richmond, with a 'crow's nest' in the top, from which it was proposed to signal over the trees covering the point, with the Admiral, which plan proved entirely successful.

"On the morning of the 15th, Lieutenants Skinner, Dean, Tenney, and Herbert, went up the levee a couple of miles to reconnoitre. They found that the enemy were crossing cavalry over from Port Hudson. Returning to the Richmond, the welcome signal-guns were heard from the Hartford, whose masts were plainly visible from the 'crow's nest.' They were quickly answered by Captain Alden, and in a few minutes the expedition started. Besides the above-mentioned officers, Mr. Shaw, acting master of the Richmond, and Mr. Gabandau, private secretary to Admiral Farragut, who came down a week ago, and returned to the Richmond from New Orleans, put in here to accompany us over. Also Mr. Graves, purser's clerk of the Albatross, accompanied the expedition. A negro was taken along as a guide. The party was well armed, and started about noon.

"They struck the woods some two miles below the river, embarked in two skiffs, and for five miles proceeded through the woods, overflowed with water to a depth ranging from three to thirty feet. It was a novel scene. Silently they paddled through the forest—the only noises heard were the voices of numberless birds and the low rustling of the leaves. Arriving near the False River, the boats were hid in the bushes, and the party waded waist-deep through the water a mile further in, where they struck the old State Levee, following which for a short distance, they came out into the open road in full sight of the enemy's batteries, which were no longer to be feared, for right ahead was the welcome sight of the flag-ship.

"The Albatross, Captain Hart, came quickly down and took us on board. While waiting for her to reach us, the enemy fired a few shells at the party, which went harmlessly over. In a few moments we were alongside the Admiral's ship, who gave us a most cordial welcome. The officiers vied with each other in making us comfortable, and eagerly asked numberless questions about the news below.

"After a good night's rest, the party, decreased by the officers belonging above, early the next morning started to return, which was a much more dangerous matter than going, for the enemy having divined our intentions, had, during the night, sent a small force over, evidently with the intention of 'gobbling' the party; but we struck a different road from the one we came on, and reached our boats in safety, having encountered but one of the enemy's pickets, who was mounted, and quickly fled on our firing at him. We got back to the Richmond at noon, having thus in twenty-four hours accomplished an object full of importance and danger, and one which Yankee pluck and perseverance alone could accomplish."

The Hartford and Albatross did excellent service in blockading the mouth of Red River, from which supplies had been sent to Vicksburg, until Admiral Porter ran by that city in May, and relieved him from this service. Admiral Farragut then returned to New Orleans, by way of the Atchafalaya, to direct the siege against Port Hudson, till its surrender to General Banks, immediately after the fall of Vicksburg.

The Admiral informs us why he went to New Orleans at the time he did, and of his ceaseless activity:

"NEW ORLEANS, *June* 29, 1863.

"While I was at Port Hudson I received a despatch stating that the rebels were in force on the west bank of the river threatening Plaquemine and Donaldsonville. I started immediately for the first-named place, but on my arrival at Baton Rouge, found a despatch from Lieutenant-Commander Weaver, to the effect that the rebels, about one hundred and fifty Texans, had made a raid into Plaquemine, some three hours previous to his arrival, and had burnt two steamers that were lying there. Lieutenant-Commander Weaver shelled the place, driving the enemy out of the town, and followed them down the river to Donaldsonville, which place he reached in advance of them; by dark I was also there, and found that the Kineo had also been sent up by Commander Morris. The enemy, finding us in such strong force of gunboats gave out that they would not attack Donaldsonville, but would go by railroad to Brashear City. I therefore ordered the Winona, Lieutenant-Commander Weaver, to cruise up and down the river, and he seeing the enemy on two occasions, shelled them.

"As I had much to attend to in New Orleans, I dropped down, placing the gunboats to the best advantage, above and below; Lieutenant-Commander Walters volunteered to assist the volunteer officer commanding the fort, in the drilling of his men at great guns. I paid them a visit and gave them my advice in case of an attack, which I looked for sooner or later. I left Commander Woolsey in the Princess Royal, in command of Donaldsonville, ordered the Winona to Plaquemine, and stationed the Kineo at a place below where the railroad ran near the river, distance about twenty-three miles from New Orleans. On the 17th instant, the enemy reached the Lafourche, crossing and attacking our pickets, who repulsed them, causing them a heavy loss. On the 18th they had a second fight and were again repulsed.

"On the 26th, the enemy, under Generals Green and Mouton, attacked and captured Brashear City. Our force there was very small. I had only a small steamer, mounting two twelve-pound howitzers, which I purchased as a tug, but I regret to say that her commander is not represented as having been any more vigilant than the rest, and backed down the bay. Mr. Ryder says, however, that he could not fire into the enemy without firing into our own people, so he withdrew and retired to New Orleans, leaving Brashear City in possession of the enemy.

"On the 27th Commander Woolsey informed me by telegraph, and Brigadier-General Emory personally, that General Green, of Texas, had notified the women and children to leave Donaldsonville, as he intended to make an attack. I immediately ordered the Kineo up to the assistance of the Princess Royal, and Lieutenant-Commander Weaver, in the Winona, being on the alert, was also at Donaldsonville in time to take part in the repulsing of the enemy. I inclose herewith Commander Woolsey's report of the affair.

"At twenty minutes past one A. M. of the 28th, the enemy made the attack, and their storming party got into the fort; but the gunboats opened a flanking fire above and below the fort, hurling destruction into the rebel ranks and driving back the supporting party, so that they broke and fled, and the twenty who entered the fort were captured. At ten minutes to five A. M., the rebels (Texans) fell back in great rage, vowing vengeance. I had in the mean time ordered up the Monongahela, Commander Read, and General Emory first, and then General Banks sent forward reëenforcements. General Stone is now in command there, and the place is perfectly secure.

"The prisoners arrived from Donaldsonville number one hundred and twenty-four—among which are one lieutenant-colonel, two majors, two captains, and five lieutenants. Our forces have buried sixty-nine rebel dead, and are still employed, calculating there are about one hundred. Colonel Phillips is among the number of the rebel dead. All of which is respectfully submitted by your obedient servant,

"D. G. FARRAGUT, Rear-Admiral."

The Mississippi was no sooner "cleared," and our Admiral *out of work* on its waters, than he looked elsewhere for a chance to deal deadly blows upon the abhorred rebellion. It was more than life to him to be in the thickest of the strife, flying at the masthead in smoke and iron hail the dear old flag, under which, while yet a boy, he fought in a distant and foreign sea.

CHAPTER XVII.

The Situation of Mobile—Preparations to attack its Fortifications—Their Strength—Generals Canby and Granger—The Advance—General Order—The Engagement—Anecdotes of the Admiral—His Report of the Splendid Affair—Thanksgiving—A Song of Victory.

THE city of Mobile is on the west side of Mobile River, at its entrance into the bay. The distance from New Orleans is one hundred and sixty miles. It came into the possession of the United States in 1813, while young Farragut was in the Essex under Captain Porter, cruising in the Pacific, and contained then only three hundred inhabitants. It grew to be the second city in importance to the cotton trade of the South, having a population of about thirty-five thousand. It was a haunt of the blockade-runners in the war, and must be taken. Admiral Farragut was the man to make the attempt to enter its waters, over which frowned the cannon of three powerful forts, Morgan, Powell, and Gaines. The enterprise had been projected before, but abandoned. The summer of 1864 found the hero of New Orleans consulting with Generals Canby and Granger. This was early in July. A few days later the plan of attack was formed, and the following spirited order issued:

"U. S. FLAG-SHIP HARTFORD, OFF MOBILE BAY, *July* 12, 1864.

"Strip your vessels and prepare for the conflict. Send down all your superfluous spars and rigging, trice up or remove the whiskers, put up the splinter nets on the starboard side, and barricade the wheel and steersmen with sails and hammocks. Lay chains or sand-bags on the deck over the machinery to resist a plunging fire. Hang the sheet chains over the side, or make any other arrangement for security that your ingenuity may suggest. Land your starboard boats, or lower and tow them on the port side, and lower the port boats down to the water's edge. Place a leadsman and the pilot in the port-quarter boat, or the one most convenient to the commander.

"The vessels will run past the forts in couples, lashed side by side, as hereinafter designated. The flag-ship will lead and steer from Sand Island N. by E. by compass, until abreast of Fort Morgan; then N. W. half N. until past the Middle Ground, then N. by W., and the others, as designated in the drawing, will follow in due order until ordered to anchor; but the bow and quarter line must be preserved, to give the chase guns a fair range; and each vessel must be kept astern of the broadside of the next ahead; each vessel will keep a very little on the starboard quarter of his next ahead, and, when abreast of the fort, will keep directly astern, and as we pass the fort will take the same distance on the port quarter of the next ahead, to enable the stern guns to fire clear of the next vessel astern.

"It will be the object of the Admiral to get as close to the fort as possible before opening fire; the ships, however, will open fire the moment the enemy opens upon us with their chase and other guns, as fast as they can be brought to bear. Use short fuses for the shell and shrapnel, and as soon as within three or four hundred yards give them grape. It is understood that heretofore we have fired too high; but with grapeshot it is necessary to elevate a little above the object, as grape will dribble from the muzzle of the gun.

"If one or more of the vessels be disabled, their partners must carry them through, if possible; but if they cannot, then the next astern must render the required assistance. But as the Admiral contemplates moving with the flood tide, it will only require sufficient power to keep the crippled vessels in the channel.

"Vessels that can must place guns upon the poop and top-gallant forecastle, and in the top on the starboard side. Should the enemy fire grape, they will remove the men from the top-gallant forecastle and poop to the guns below until out of grape range. The howitzers must keep up a constant fire from the time they can reach with shrapnel until out of its range.

"D. G. FARRAGUT,
"Rear-Admiral Commanding W. G. B. Squadron."

A single fact sheds further light on his comprehensive ability for so daring an assault upon defences combining all the perils to the invading force that engineering skill could construct. He determined to go in with the strong flood tide, because, in case a vessel was hit and partially disabled, it would not stop and drift astern, but must float onwards into and with the fight. In his triumph at New Orleans, Port Hudson, and Vicksburg, almost the greatest difficulty which he had encountered was the rapidity and adverse force of the Mississippi current. If a vessel was hit it had to drift astern into the fire, or out of the circle of service. This he felt would never do, and the result shows how correct was his judgment. With the flood every ship made its way into the bay; and the Oneida, which was last, realized that its position on the rear was the most serious one, since the forts, silenced by the sustained fire of the whole line, reopened upon the sternmost vessel, when the weight and frequency of the leading vessels' broadsides had slackened. "Farragut, in assuming the lead, demonstrated the truth of a military aphorism, that audacity and presence of mind constitute armor and arms of proof."

There was a pleasant incident on the eve of battle illustrative of the Admiral's character. The men of the Hartford tell a good story of him. They came aft in a body the night before the attack on Fort Morgan, and through their petty officers requested of the captain of the Hartford to see the Admiral. When he came out they asked him if they could have some grog before going into action the next day. "I have no particular objection to your having a little grog," he calmly replied, "if there is any on board; but I have been to sea a good deal, and have seen some fighting, but *I have never seen the time when I needed rum to help me do my duty.* I will order for you two pots of hot coffee at two o'clock to-morrow morning, and at eight o'clock I will pipe you to breakfast in Mobile Bay."

Of the entire achievement the Admiral shall tell his own story, and it is not often that the official reports of commanding officers, necessarily giving the details of the conflicts, will interest the youthful reader; but General Sherman's and Admiral Farragut's despatches are exceptions in this respect. The forcible and often graphic statements reveal the cultivated genius which can wield the pen with skill and point equal to that displayed in handling the sword. For this reason I shall add to the sketch of the "glorious victory" Farragut's peculiar and striking account of what he did and saw. Even boys will catch the *ring* of the battle itself, and say with another, "How well he writes after fighting so well!" You will pause with moistened eye over his allusion to the wounded prisoners, and the lamented Craven:

"U. S. Flag-ship Hartford, Mobile Bay, *August* 12, 1864.

"Sir:—I had the honor to forward the Department on the evening of the 5th instant a report of my *entrée* into Mobile Bay on the morning of that day, and which, though brief, contained all the principal facts of the attack. Notwithstanding the loss of life, particularly on this ship, and the terrible disaster to the Tecumseh, the result of the fight was a glorious victory; and I have reason to feel proud of the officers, seamen, and marines of the squadron under my command, for it has never fallen to the lot of an officer to be thus situated and thus sustained. Regular discipline will bring men to any amount of endurance, but there is a natural fear of hidden dangers, particularly when so awfully destructive of human life as the torpedo, which requires more than discipline to overcome.

"Preliminary to a report of the action of the 5th, I desire to call the attention of the Department to the previous steps taken in consultation with Generals Canby and Granger on the 8th of July. I had an interview with these officers on board the Hartford, on the subject of an attack upon Forts Morgan and Gaines, at which it was agreed that General Canby would send all the troops he could spare to coöperate with the fleet. Circumstances soon obliged General Canby to inform me that he could not despatch a sufficient number to invest both forts, and in reply, I suggested that Gaines should be the first invested, engaging to have a force in the sound ready to protect the landing of the army on Dauphin Island in the rear of that fort, and I assigned Lieutenant-Commander De Krafft, of the Conemaugh, to that duty.

"On the 1st instant General Granger visited me again on the Hartford. In the mean time the Tecumseh had arrived at Pensacola, and Captain Craven informed me that he would be ready in four days for any service. We therefore fixed upon the 4th of August as the day for the landing of the troops, and my entrance into the bay, but owing to delays mentioned in Captain Jenkins' communication to me, the Tecumseh was not ready. General Granger, however, to my mortification, was up to the time, and the troops actually landed on Dauphin Island.

"As subsequent events proved, the delay turned to our advantage, as the rebels were busily engaged during the 4th in throwing troops and supplies into Fort Gaines, all of which were captured a few days afterwards. The Tecumseh arrived on the evening of the 4th, and every thing being propitious, I proceeded to the attack on the following morning. As mentioned in my previous despatch, the vessels outside the bar which were designed to participate in the engagement, were all under way by forty minutes past five in the morning, in the following order, two abreast and lashed together:

"Brooklyn, Captain James Alden, with the Octorara, Lieutenant-Commander C. H. Green, on the port side.

"Hartford, Captain Percival Drayton, with the Metacomet, Lieutenant-Commander J. E. Jouett.

"Richmond, Captain T. A. Jenkins, with the Port Royal, Lieutenant-Commander B. Gherardi.

"Lackawanna, Captain J. B. Marchand, with the Seminole, Commander E. Donaldson.

"Monongahela, Commander J. H. Strong, with the Kennebec, Lieutenant-Commander W. P. McCann.

"Ossipee, Commander W. E. LeRoy, with the Itasca, Lieutenant-Commander George Brown.

"Oneida, Commander J. R. M. Mullany, with the Galena, Lieutenant-Commander C. H. Wells.

"The iron-clads Tecumseh, Commander T. A. M. Craven, the Manhattan, Commander J. W. A. Nicholson, the Winnebago, Commander T. H. Stevens, and the Chickasaw, Lieutenant-Commander T. H. Perkins, were already ahead inside the bar, and had been ordered to take up their positions on the starboard side of the wooden ships, or between them and Fort Morgan, for the double purpose of keeping down the fire from the water battery and the parapet guns of the fort, as well as to attack the ram Tennessee as soon as the fort was passed. It was only at the urgent request of the captains and commanding officers that I yielded to the Brooklyn being the leading ship of the line, as she had four chase guns and an ingenious arrangement for picking up torpedoes, and because in their judgment the flag-ship ought not to be too much exposed. This I believe to be an error ; for apart from the fact that exposure is one of the penalties of rank in the navy, it will always be the aim of the enemy to destroy the flag-ship, and, as will appear in the sequel, such attempt was very persistently made, but Providence did not permit it to be successful.

"The attacking fleet steamed steadily up the main ship channel, the Tecumseh firing the first shot at 6:47. At six minutes past seven the fort opened upon us, and was replied to by a gun from the Brooklyn, and immediately after the action became general. It was soon apparent that there was some difficulty ahead. The Brooklyn, for some cause which I did not then clearly understand, but which has since been explained by Captain Alden in his report, arrested the advance of the whole fleet, while at the same time the guns of the fort were playing with great effect upon that vessel and the Hartford. A moment after I saw the Tecumseh, struck by a torpedo, disappear almost instantaneously beneath the waves, carrying with her her gallant commander and nearly all her crew. I determined at once, as I had originally intended, to take the lead, and after ordering the Metacomet to send a boat to save if possible any of the perishing crew, I dashed ahead with the Hartford, and the ships followed on, their officers believing that they were going to a noble death with their commander-in-chief. I steamed through between the buoys where the torpedoes were supposed to have been sunk. These buoys had been previously examined by my flag-lieutenant, J. Crittenden Watson, in several night reconnoissances. Though he had not been able to discover the sunken torpedoes, yet we had been assured by refugees, deserters, and others, of their existence; but believing that from their having been some time in the water they were probably innocuous, I determined to take the chance of their explosion.

"From the moment I turned to the northwestward to clear the middle ground, we were enabled to keep such a broadside fire upon the batteries of Fort Morgan that their guns did us comparatively little injury. Just after we passed the fort, which was about ten minutes before eight o'clock, the ram Tennessee dashed out at this ship, as had been expected, and in anticipation of which I had ordered the monitors on our starboard side. I took no further notice of her than to return her fire. The rebel gunboats Morgan, Gaines, and Selma, were ahead, and the latter particularly annoyed us with a raking fire, which our guns could not return. At two minutes after eight o'clock I ordered the Metacomet to cast off and go in pursuit of the Selma. Captain Jouett was after her in a moment, and in an hour's time he had her as a prize. She was commanded by P. N. Murphy, formerly of the United States Navy. He was wounded in the wrist; his executive officer, Lieutenant Comstock, and eight of the crew killed, and seven or eight wounded. Lieutenant-Commander Jouett's conduct during the whole affair commands my warmest commendations. The Morgan and Gaines succeeded in escaping under the protection of the guns of Fort Morgan, which would have been prevented had the other gunboats been as prompt in their movements as the Metacomet. The want of pilots, however, I believe, was the principal difficulty. The Gaines was so injured by our fire that she had to be run ashore, where she was subsequently destroyed, but the Morgan escaped to Mobile during the night, though she was chased and fired upon by our cruisers.

"Having passed the forts and dispersed the enemy's gunboats, I had ordered most of the vessels to anchor, when I perceived the ram Tennessee standing up for this ship; this was at forty-five minutes past eight. I was not long in comprehending his intentions to be the destruction of the flag-ship. The monitors and such of the wooden vessels as I thought best adapted for the purpose, were immediately ordered to attack the ram, not only with their guns but bows on at full speed. And then began one of the fiercest naval combats on record. The Monongahela, Commander Strong, was the first vessel that struck her, and in doing so carried away his own iron prow, together with the cutwater, without apparently doing his adversary much injury. The Lackawanna, Captain Marchand, was the next vessel to strike her, which she did at full speed; but though her stern was cut and crushed to the plank ends for the distance of three feet above the water's edge to five feet below, the only perceptible effect on the ram was to give her a heavy lift. The Hartford was the third vessel which struck her, but as the Tennessee quickly shifted her helm, the blow was a glancing one, and as she rasped along our side we poured our whole port broadside of 9-inch solid shot within ten feet of her casemate. The monitors worked slowly, but delivered their fire as opportunity offered. The Chickasaw succeeded in getting under her stern, and a 15-inch shot from the Manhattan broke through her iron plating and heavy wooden backing, though the missile itself did not enter the vessel.

"Immediately after the collision with the flag-ship, I directed Captain Drayton to bear down for the ram again. He was doing so at full speed, when, unfortunately, the Lackawanna ran into the Hartford just forward of the mizzen-mast, cutting her down to within two feet of the water's edge. We soon got clear again, however, and were fast approaching our adversary, when she struck her colors and ran up the white flag. She was at this time sore beset: the Chickasaw was pounding away at her stern, the Ossipee was approaching her at full speed, and the Monongahela, Lackawanna, and this ship were bearing down upon her, determined upon her destruction. Her smoke-stack had been shot away, her steering-chains were gone, compelling a resort to her relieving tackles, and several of the port-shutters were jammed. Indeed, from the time the Hartford struck her until her surrender, she never fired a gun. As the Ossipee, Commander Le Roy, was about to strike her, she hoisted the white flag, and that vessel immediately stopped her engine, though not in time to avoid a glancing blow. During the contest with the rebel gunboats and the ram Tennessee, and which terminated by her surrender at ten o'clock, we lost many more men than from the fire of the batteries of Fort Morgan. Admiral Buchanan was wounded in the leg, two or three of his men were killed, and five or six wounded. Commander Johnston, formerly of the U. S. Navy, was in command of the Tennessee, and came on board the flag-ship to surrender his sword and that of Admiral Buchanan. The Surgeon, Dr. Conrad, came with him, stated the condition of the Admiral, and wished to know what was to be done with him. Fleet-Surgeon Palmer, who was on board the Hartford during the action, commiserating the sufferings of the wounded, suggested that those of both sides be sent to Pensacola, where they could be properly cared for. I therefore addressed a note to Brigadier-General R. L. Page, commanding Fort Morgan, informing him that Admiral Buchanan and others of the

Tennessee had been wounded, and desiring to know whether he would permit one of our vessels under a flag of truce to convey them with, or without, our men wounded to Pensacola, on the understanding that the vessel would take out none but the wounded, and bring nothing back that she did not take out. This was acceded to by General Page, and the Metacomet proceeded on this mission of humanity.

"As I had an elevated position in the main rigging near the top, I was able to overlook not only the deck of the Hartford, but the other vessels of the fleet. I witnessed the terrible effects of the enemy's shot and the good conduct of the men at their guns; and although no doubt their hearts sickened, as mine did, when their shipmates were struck down beside them, yet there was not a moment's hesitation to lay their comrades aside and spring again to their deadly work. Our little consort, the Metacomet, was also under my immediate eye during the whole action up to the moment I ordered her to cast off in pursuit of the Selma. The coolness and promptness of Lieutenant-Commander Jouett throughout merit high praise; his whole conduct was worthy of his reputation. In this connection, I must not omit to call the attention of the Department to the conduct of Acting Ensign Henry C. Nields, of the Metacomet, who had charge of the boat sent from that vessel when the Tecumseh sunk. He took her in under one of the most galling fires I ever saw, and succeeded in rescuing from death ten of her crew within 600 yards of the fort. I would respectfully recommend his advancement. The commanding officers of all the vessels who took part in the action deserve my warmest commendations, not only for the untiring zeal with which they had prepared their ships for the contest, but for their skill and daring in carrying out my orders during the engagement. With the exception of the momentary arrest of the fleet when the Hartford passed ahead, and to which I have already adverted, the order of battle was preserved, and the ships followed each other in close order past the batteries of Fort Morgan, and in comparative safety, too, with the exception of the Oneida. Her boilers were penetrated by a shot from the fort which completely disabled her, but her consort, the Galena, firmly fastened to her side, brought her safely through, showing clearly the wisdom of the precaution of carrying the vessels in two abreast. Commander Mullany, who had solicited eagerly to take part in the action, was severely wounded, losing his left arm. In the encounter with the ram, the commanding officers obeyed with alacrity the order to run her down, and without hesitation exposed their ships to destruction to destroy the enemy. Our iron-clads, from their slow speed and bad steering, had some difficulty in getting into and maintaining their position in line as we passed the fort, and in the subsequent encounter with the Tennessee, from the same causes were not so effective as could have been desired; but I cannot give too much praise to Lieutenant-Commander Perkins, who, though he had orders from the Department to return North, volunteered to take command of the Chickasaw, and did his duty nobly.

"The Winnebago was commanded by Commander T. H. Stevens, who volunteered for that position. His vessel steers very badly, and neither of his turrets will work, which compelled him to turn his vessel every time to get a shot, so that he could not fire very often, but he did the best under the circumstances.

"The Manhattan appeared to work well, though she moved slowly. Commander Nicholson delivered his fire deliberately, and, as before stated, with one of his 15-inch shot broke through the armor of the Tennessee, with its wooden backing, though the shot itself did not enter the vessel. No other shot broke through her armor, though many of her plates were started, and several of her port-shutters jammed by the fire from the different ships.

"The Hartford, my flag-ship, was commanded by Captain Percival Drayton, who exhibited throughout that coolness and ability for which he has been long known to his brother officers. But I must speak of that officer in a double capacity. He is the fleet-captain of my squadron, and one of more determined energy, untiring devotion to duty, and zeal for the service, tempered by great calmness, I do not think adorns any navy. I desire to call your attention to this officer, though well aware that in thus speaking of his high qualities I am only communicating officially to the Department that which it knew full well before. To him, and to my staff in their respective positions, I am indebted for the detail of my fleet.

"Lieutenant J. Crittenden Watson, my flag-lieutenant, has been brought to your notice in former despatches. During the action he was on the poop attending to the signals, and performed his duties as might be expected—thoroughly. He is a scion worthy the noble stock he sprang from, and I commend him to your attention. My secretary, Mr. McKinley, and acting ensign E. H. Brownell, were also on the poop, the latter taking notes of the action, a duty which he performed with coolness and accuracy.

"Two other acting ensigns of my staff (Mr. Bogart and Mr. Heginbotham) were on duty in the powder division, and, as the reports will show, exhibited zeal and ability. The latter, I regret to say, was severely wounded by a raking shot from the Tennessee when we collided with that vessel, and died a few hours after. Mr. Heginbotham was a young married man, and has left a widow and one child, whom I commend to the kindness of the Department.

"Lieutenant A. R. Yates, of the Augusta, acted as an additional aide to me on board the Hartford, and was very efficient in the transmission of orders. I have given him the command, temporarily, of the captured steamer Selma.

"The last of my staff, and to whom I would call the notice of the Department, is not the least in importance. I mean Pilot Martin Freeman. He has been my great reliance in all difficulties in his line of duty. During the action he was in the main-top, piloting the ships into the bay. He was cool and brave throughout, never losing his self-possession. This man was captured early in the war in a fine fishing smack which he owned, and, though he protested that he had no interest in the war, and only asked for the privilege of fishing for the fleet, yet his services were too valuable to the captors as a pilot not to be secured. He was appointed a first-class pilot, and has served us with zeal and fidelity, and has lost his vessel, which went to pieces on Ship Island. I commend him to the Department.

"It gives me pleasure to refer to several officers who volunteered to take any situation where they might be useful, some of whom were on their way North, either by orders of the Department or condemned by medical survey. The reports of different commanders will show how they conducted themselves.

"I have already mentioned Lieutenant-Commander Perkins, of the Chickasaw, and Lieutenant Yates, of the Augusta. Acting volunteer Lieutenant William Hamilton, late commanding officer of the Augusta Dinsmore, had been invalided by medical survey, but he eagerly offered his services on board the iron-clad Chickasaw, having had much experience in our monitors.

"Acting volunteer Lieutenant P. Giraud, another experienced officer in iron-clads, asked to go in one of these vessels, but as they were all well supplied with officers I permitted him to go on the Ossipee, under Commander Le Roy. After the action, he was given temporary charge of the ram Tennessee.

"Before closing this report, there is one other officer of my squadron of whom I feel bound to speak, Captain T. A. Jenkins, of the Richmond, who was formerly my chief of staff, not because of his having held that position, but because he never forgets to do his duty to the Government, and takes now the same interest in the fleet as when he stood in that relation to me. He is also the commanding officer of the second division of my squadron, and, as such, has shown ability and the most untiring zeal. He carries out the spirit of one of Lord Collingwood's best sayings: 'Not to be afraid of doing too much; those who are, seldom do as much as they ought.' When in Pensacola he spent days on the bar, placing the buoys in the best positions; was always looking after the interests of the service, and keeping the vessels from being detained one moment longer in ports than was necessary. The gallant Craven told me only the night before the action in which he lost his life: 'I regret, Admiral, that

I have detained you; but had it not been for Captain Jenkins, God knows when I should have been here. When your order came, I had not received an ounce of coal!'

"I feel that I should not be doing my duty did I not call the attention of the Department to an officer who has performed all his various duties with so much zeal and fidelity.

"Very respectfully, your obedient servant,

"D. G. FARRAGUT,

"*Rear-Admiral, Commanding W. G. Squadron.*"

There was a fact in the engagement which indicates the depth of attachment cherished toward the "Old Salamander," as he was familiarly called by his brave "boys." When the Hartford retired from the first onset upon the rebel flag-ship Tennessee, and got ready to dash the second time against the enemy, suddenly she was herself struck with tremendous power by one of our own vessels moving down upon the same defiant leviathan of treason. There was a fearful crash, and the alarm spread among the loyal seamen for the Admiral's safety.

Above the roar and din of the strife rose the voices of loyal, devoted men, "The Admiral! the Admiral! Save the Admiral! Get the Admiral out of the ship!" All thought of personal safety was lost in the intense anxiety of those brave hearts for their noble commander. Sublimely beautiful illustration of unselfish, merited devotion, amid the flying shot which imperilled every life! It was a crisis of thrilling interest.

It soon became apparent that the Hartford would survive the shock, and, though shattered and quivering under the blow, continue to float. To keep above water was enough for the untrembling hero; and turning to his valiant fleet-captain, his order was: "Go on with speed! Ram her again!" And on the Hartford went, to conquer or go down. Just before she reached the Tennessee the white flag was run up, and the enemy was ours! With such a glorious leader, who declares that God is his leader, success must wait upon action.

"The moral of the fight in Mobile is—'Get close to your enemy;' the nearer the better, the nearer the safer. The rebels imagined that the ship channel leading so very close to the powerful Fort Morgan, no ships would dare attempt the passage; or, if the attempt were made, none would succeed, But in Farragut's hands this peculiarity of the channel became an advantage to the attacking, and a weakness to the defending side. He carried his flag-ship, the Hartford, close as possible to the stone walls, and instead of trying to batter them down with heavy shot, actually drove the gunners from their guns by well-directed volleys of grape and canister. This would be almost incredible; but if it were not true our fleet could not have passed the fort and water battery with so little injury as it received.

"The novel and ingenious expedient of lashing his vessels together, two and two, showed how thoroughly the Rear-Admiral had considered the dangers in his way, and how successfully he met them. First: if the exposed half of his fleet had been disabled, the other half would still have gone in with but little injury. Second: his battle line was not liable to disorganization, by any vessel dropping out, and perhaps fouling another. The Oneida was disabled, but her consort pulled her through, and the Oneida's men did not even leave their guns. Third: if any vessel had been sunk, her consort would have surely and quickly have saved the crew. Fourth: his battle-line was shortened by half, and the passage of course robbed of half its risks to the fleet. These were the chief points gained by Farragut's admirable and novel disposition of his force.

"Farragut stood, high above the smoke of battle, in the main-top, lashed there that he might not be dashed from his perch by the shock of concussion with the enemy's ships. From there he had a clear view of the field, and was able to give his orders with precision and certainty. It will not have escaped the reader's attention, that, though the Admiral did not, for sufficient reasons, place his own ship in the van of the battle in passing the forts, no sooner did an accident cause the Brooklyn to slow, than he ordered the Hartford to pass her, and lead the advance."

It was one of the grandest spectacles ever witnessed in battle, when, lashed to masts, the admiral looked down from his exposed watch-tower upon the fiercely raging contest. It made his men wild with enthusiasm, and will always be admired while heroism is dear to the people.

At length the news reached England, and the *Times* and *Naval Journal* thus replied to the thunder of Farragut's war-ships:

"Admiral Farragut has been the most successful of all the Federal officers. His achievement in the present case is, as we have said, precisely similar to his operations at New Orleans, although the struggle in this instance has been far more severe. In both cases he has run the gauntlet of forts supported by a fleet. At New Orleans the Confederates were very ill prepared; but his success in the present instance, against what we may suppose to be the matured defences of two forts, cannot but be instructive to us at a time when we are occupied with a scientific contest between ships and guns. It would seem that where the passage of a fleet cannot be obstructed, it can always run the gauntlet of forts at the expense of a certain amount of loss. The defeat of the Federals before Charleston has principally arisen from the facility with which the Confederates have obstructed the channels, and have thus been able to detain the Federal fleet under the fire of their forts. We shall look with interest for the details of this engagement, in the expectation that they will throw some light on this disputed point of naval warfare."

"Whatever speculations may have been sent abroad concerning the value of Farragut's success in forcing the forts at the entrance to Mobile Bay, there can now be no doubt of the signal character of his victory, and of the serious blow given to the Confederates in that quarter. It was argued that he had done nothing more than run past Fort Gaines and Fort Morgan, and sink and destroy a certain number of the enemy's fleet; that his position was most precarious, as his transports could not pass the batteries, and that he would have to run back again for supplies; that he could not get up to the town in consequence of shoal water and of formidable works on land; and that he could not hope to hold his own, as he had no troops to make an impression on the sides of the bay, and prevent the transmission of supplies to the forts at the entrance. Yesterday's news blew all these speculations, arguments, and assertions into the air, with one exception. By the surrender of Fort Gaines on the west side of the entrance, and by the voluntary destruction of Fort Powell on Dauphin Island, the position of Farragut is rendered secure. The middle channel is left open, and stores can be landed under the guns of Fort Gaines; and the channel to New Orleans, which was closed by Fort Powell, near Grant's Pass, must now fall into the hands of the victors. How far Mobile is itself in danger must depend on the power of the Federal Government to send such an army there as may assist and cover the flotilla in its future operations. On the west side the city is reported to be defended by very heavy earthworks and batteries; and on the Dog River bar, just below the city, there is a line of sunken vessels. On the east side there are few works, but the city is defended there by the Tensas River, and by the deep, broad, and rapid Alabama. However, on that side lies Pensacola, and, if the Federals can assemble an army there to march straight on the east side of the city, whilst another force approaches and invests the west side, the Confederates will be hard set to hold their own. They must collect an army to defend the city, which is now between four hostile points—New Orleans to the west, Sherman's army to the north, Farragut's fleet to south, and Pensacola to the east. Next to New Orleans, the city of Mobile was the greatest cotton port in the State. It was lately driving a considerable trade in blockade-running, and gave abundant supplies to the Confederacy. Now, neither can cotton go out nor goods run in, and Mobile, its inhabitants, and garrison, are thrown on the resources of the impoverished and hard-pressed Confederacy."

"T" has celebrated the victory in a beautiful poem:

"MOBILE BAY.

The sea upon the bar is smooth,
Yet perilous the path
Where Gaines' and Morgan's bristling guns
Belch forth their rebel wrath.
And, close beyond, their iron-clads
Loom in the breaking day;
But FARRAGUT is leading us,
And we will clear the way.

Fast flew the shot, fierce shrieked the shell;
Thundered our broadsides back;
It seemed the very fires of hell
Were bursting o'er our track.
But steady, onward, pressed our ships,
Careless of hurtling death,
Till the broad waters of the bay
Gave us a space for breath.

One ship was lost—our wooden-walls
Defied the walls of stone,
And, proudly sailing by, gave back
The greetings fiercely thrown;
But, 'neath a Monitor, burst forth
Flame from the treach'rous wave:
In that fell flash, staunch ship and crew
Sank to an ocean grave.

Our task is but begun;—see where
The rebel monsters ride,

In armor clad of matchless proof,
  Vauntful in untamed pride.
They long have been the rebel boast,
  Monarchs of all their kind;
Shot fly their adamantine sides,
  Their rush is like the wind.

Oh, helpless seem our oaken hulls,
  Powerless each well-tried gun:
The rebel, in his pride, believes
  The fight already won.
But gallant souls are panic proof,
  In God their hopeful trust,—
Spirit is mightier than flesh—
  Soul than its casing dust.

Again our VIKING leads the way;
  Glorious the sailor pride
With which our wooden-walls dash on
  To perils all untried.
Whilst, confident in iron strength,
  The rebel monsters leap,
To crush us 'neath their iron prows,
  And whelm us in the deep.

Close quarters now; we cannot fend
  The blows that on us rain;
Our only wish—our only thought—
  To deal them back again.
Our muzzles touch their iron sides,
  Our ports alive with flame;
Hurrah! our thunderbolts, close driv'n,
  Crash through the armored frame.

We heed not though our comrades fall
  Like leaves at Winter's breath;
Drunk with the glorious battle-rage,
  We lead the Dance of Death.
Berserkars all, we little reck
  Whom ODIN's choice may be;
The carnage only fires our hearts
  Fiercer for victory.

We triumph!—see the traitor flag
  Is doused—the white one flies;
The rebel admiral has struck;
  Conquered the monster lies;
A second yields, whilst far away
  The others wildly flee.
Hurrah! our wooden-walls have swept
  The Cyclops from the sea.

Thanks be to God! for in His strength
  We won the glorious fight:
May He receive our comrades brave
  Who bade the world good night.
And may our people oft recall,
  Through many a happy day,
The men who fought with FARRAGUT
  In bloody Mobile Bay.

August 5, 1864."

CHAPTER XVIII.

The National Joy—The President's Thanks—Congressional Action—Other Voices of Gladness—Leave of Absence—Arrival at New York—The Welcome—Is created Vice-Admiral.

THE "great naval victory" thrilled the nation's heart with almost the intensity of joy that the fall of Vicksburg did. Both places had long held the public eye, and much of war's resources had been expended upon them when they yielded to Yankee prowess. The President issued the following despatch:

"EXECUTIVE MANSION, *September* 3.

"The national thanks are tendered by the President to Admiral Farragut and Major-General Canby for the skill and harmony with which the recent operations in Mobile harbor and against Fort Powell, Fort Gaines, and Fort Morgan, were planned and carried into execution.

"Also, to Admiral Farragut and Major-General Granger, under whose immediate command they were conducted, and to the gallant commanders on sea and land, and to the sailors and soldiers engaged in the operations, for their energy and courage, which, under the blessing of Providence, have been crowned with brilliant success, and have won for them the applause and thanks of the nation. ABRAHAM LINCOLN."

Congress united in the expression of grateful admiration toward our heroes, in resolutions of a similar character. In giving utterance to the popular gladness, the *Army and Navy Journal* well said: "Rear-Admiral Farragut has added another red-letter day to our naval calendar. The 5th of August will be 'kept' by old salts, in years to come, as commemorating one of the proudest and most daring achievements of our own or any other navy. Just as some of our old commodores, veterans of the last war with Great Britain, would put on their fighting coats, and fight the battle over again on the anniversary of some one of Perry's, or Decatur's, or Hull's famous victories, so will the veterans of this war, in years to come, celebrate the passage of the Mississippi forts, and the victory in Mobile Bay. Nor will they need to boast over their grog—for the plainest and baldest story of these battles will excite the wonder and admiration of the listening youngsters.

"In the attack on the forts and fleet of Mobile, Farragut has displayed the same rare combination of qualities for which he first became generally known by the brilliant passage of the Mississippi forts. In both these actions he showed himself as audacious as though he had not a grain of sense, and as prudent as though he had not a spark of audacity. He is as great in preparation as in action; he makes such novel and admirable use of his means as to baffle all the plans of the enemy; and having prepared himself with all the patience of the merest plodder, he delivers battle with an impetuosity which breaks down all resistance.

"In many of his qualities Farragut resembles Lord Dundonald, the bravest and truest of British seamen; the Englishman, above all others, dear to the hearts of British seamen. It requires a man of Farragut's genius and unconquerable pluck, a man who, to quote the words of the Secretary of the Navy, is willing to take great risks in order to accomplish great results. Tennesseeans may be proud that their State has produced two such men as Andrew Jackson and D. G. Farragut.

"Let us hope that Congress will at its next session provide a proper reward for the old hero, to whom we owe two such brilliant and important victories. Rear-Admiral is at present the highest grade in our navy. It is an absurd designation, to be at the head; and we cannot think it would have been declared such had not the Naval Committees intended to leave the opportunity open to create the higher grade which the title *Rear*-Admiral supposes.

It is not our custom to reward with grants of money, or with titles, the great achievements of the nation's leaders. But it is fit that such services as Farragut has rendered, and as others may render, should receive the acknowledgment which sailors and soldiers prize—an advance in rank. We have now the grade of Lieutenant-General in the army; and Farragut has given cause for the establishment of equal grade in the navy."

The veteran hero continued to command the Gulf Squadron during the subsequent weeks of comparative rest, till, feeling the need of a furlough, he was granted leave of absence for three months. He immediately took a warm adieu of his brave men, with the exception of those who accompanied him in the flag-ship Hartford.

"The Hartford sailed from Pensacola November 20th, reaching Key West December 4th, and on the 8th encountering a terrible gale, which continued for two days. On the 12th she dropped her anchor off New York. The following is her list of officers, and the story of the Admiral's reception:

"Rear-Admiral—David G. Farragut.

"Captain—Percival Drayton.

"Lieutenant-Commander—Lewis A. Kimberly.

"Lieutenants, J. Crittendon Watson, H. B. Tyson, La Rue P. Adams; Ensigns, Wm. H. Whiting, G. B. D. Glidden; Acting Master's Mates, George R. Avery, W. H. Hathorne, J. J. Tinell, James Morgan, Chas. Brown;

Boatswain, Robert Dixon; Gunner, John S. Staples; Acting Vol. Lieutenant, George G. Upham; Surgeon, Phillip Lansdale; Assistant Surgeon, Wm. Commons; Paymaster, Wm. T. Meredith; Chief Engineer, Thomas Williamson; First Assistant Engineers, E. B. Hatch, F. A. Wilson; Second Assistant Engineers, Isaac De Graff, H. L. Pickington; Third Assistant Engineer, James E. Speights; Secretary to Commander of Squadron, Alex'r McKinley; Acting Ensign to Commander of Squadron, Wm. Bourne; Paymaster's Clerk, Horatio A. Wood; Carpenter, Hiram L. Dixon; Sailmaker, Theodore C. Herbert; Captain of Marines, Charles Heywood.

"The committee, to whom had been assigned the task of welcoming the Hartford and her commander, proceeded to the foot of Broadway at 11½ o'clock, and thence embarked on board Captain Constable's revenue cutter Bronx, which Collector Draper had kindly afforded for the occasion. Accompanying the collector were Messrs. Francis Skiddy, Isaac Bell, Mr. Stewart, the Assistant Treasurer, and other prominent citizens. There was considerable uncertainty as to the arrival of the Hartford, but it was the fixed determination of Collector Draper to make the trip, in order that the gallant conqueror of Fort Morgan should be met with welcome at the very mouth of our harbor, or beyond.

"At 1½ o'clock, however, the anxiety of all on board was relieved by the intelligence that the Hartford was in sight, and coming up the outer bay. Before this, however, it had been ascertained from the bark Australian, which was spoken off Staten Island, that the Hartford was at the bar, with Admiral Farragut on board. All haste was now made to reach the Hartford, and when but a slight interval remained between the two vessels, Admiral Farragut and Captain Drayton appeared on their poop-deck, and exchanged friendly salutations with the party on board the cutter. Enthusiastic cheers were given by those on board the ships. The latter came on the starboard side of the flag-ship, at whose mizzen-mast flaunted the blue pennant of the Admiral. The committee, and others, on stepping on board the flag-ship, were heartily greeted by her commander, when the whole party proceeded down into the principal cabin. After having taken seats, and preliminary introductions being concluded, Collector Draper arose and spoke as follows:

"'Admiral Farragut: It becomes my pleasing duty to inform you, on behalf of a committee which we here represent that arrangements have been made to tender to you a reception somewhat worthy of your great services to the country; and in order that I may perform my duty acceptably to the gentlemen who commissioned me, I have to state that they are ready to give you a cordial welcome on your arrival in the city. They fully appreciate the honors which you have bestowed on the flag and the country, which you have so often successfully defended.

You justly hold a prominent place in the affections of the city, which is preëminently proud of your services. On your arrival you will be received by a meeting of the leading citizens, who will be ready to congratulate you on your visit to the city, and to show their appreciation of your great efforts in support of the nation.'

"The Collector then read the resolutions adopted at the meeting in the Astor House relative to the Admiral, and closed by expressing the pleasure he experienced at being delegated with the other members of the committee to escort the Admiral to this city.

"The Admiral responded very briefly indeed. He felt bound to return to the committee his sincere thanks for the manner in which his services were spoken of by them, and believed the consideration was applicable to his command. He had done no more than his duty, and felt deeply grateful for the tokens of appreciation he had received.

"During the friendly intercourse that followed, the Admiral pointed out several curiosities that he had on board his ship. Among these were two chairs, placed in his cabin, one of which formerly belonged to the rebel General Page, and the other to Admiral Buchanan, which latter had been taken from the Tennessee. On the back of the first was the inscription, 'Brig.-Gen. Page, August 23, 1864,' and on the second, 'Admiral Buchanan, August 6, 1864.' The iron-clad Dictator, bound in from her trial trip, passed within a few yards of the Hartford. The crews of both vessels cheered loudly. On nearing Governor's Island the steamer Henry Burden came alongside, and sent on board General Van Vliet and Colonel Clitz, who paid their respects to Admiral Farragut. The French steamer Tysephone, which lay in the vicinity, dipped her colors three times in compliment to the Admiral, and her commander also came on board. When opsite the Battery the Hartford was anchored, when the Bronx came alongside, and taking the Admiral and entire company on board, landed them.

"Much curiosity was manifested by members of the committee with regard to the vessel which has become so famous during the war. Her decks were tidy enough, but her rigging and spars bore testimony, from their weather-worn appearance, to the severity of the storm they have recently withstood; while, perhaps, an observant eye might have detected indications of sterner strife than that of the elements—the freshly mended battle-scars which paint could not wholly hide.

"In personal appearance, Admiral Farragut would suggest to the minds of the many the 'Sir Gervais Oaks' of Cooper's novel of the 'Two Admirals.' Hale, hearty, and of rather spare but powerful mould, the hero of New Orleans and Mobile Bay is apparently between fifty and sixty years of age. He looks as if he dearly loved a joke, steps with the springiness of a boy, and his manner is so perfectly frank and unassuming that it is no wonder that he is beloved by his officers and men.

"It was about 3¼ o'clock when the revenue cutter Bronx, with Messrs. Moses Taylor, Sloane, and a few other gentlemen of the committee, started a second time from her dock at the Battery, for Mrs. Admiral Farragut's 'dear old Hartford,' which, by this time, had come to anchorage in the harbor. She was soon reached, and Admiral Farragut, accompanied by Captain Drayton, Collector Draper, General Van Vliet, and several officers of the ship, descended to the deck of the Bronx; while the Hartford saluted with a discharge of both broadsides. The cutter pushed off, and the party descended to her cabin, where the short interval of the passage to the shore was occupied in a social, chatty way, the Admiral appearing in a most excellent humor, but having little to say, and apparently somewhat disconcerted at the number of eyes that were fastened upon his face. But a few moments had elapsed since the appearance of the gallant Hartford in the harbor was generally known, but, nevertheless, quite a throng collected at the dock, awaiting the arrival of the cutter, and anxiously trying to catch a glimpse of the hero of Mobile. Cheer after cheer arose as he stepped on the pier, and before reaching terra firma the crowd had increased to hundreds, and the Admiral had to run a gauntlet of outstretched, welcoming hands, which he good-humoredly shook to the best of his ability, before reaching the coach which was in waiting. In this he at length found refuge, accompanied by Collector Draper, and drove toward the Custom House, followed by an omnibus filled with the remainder of the *suite*. The crowd was soon left behind, and probably but few of them knew that the simple hack which drove so rapidly up Broadway and down Wall Street, contained the distinguished personages which it did until its arrival. Here another crowd, wild with enthusiasm, was so quickly collected that it was with difficulty that the party, with the old hero in their midst, and followed by a press of solid citizens, could penetrate up stairs to the Collector's room. This was, however, at length reached, but filled, almost as soon, to suffocation with the eager crowd, but a small space being reserved for the Admiral, Messrs. Draper, Taylor, and a few others. Among the notables present were General John Cochrane, General Wetmore, the Hon. Hiram Walbridge, Assistant-Treasurer Stewart, and a great many others."

Collector Draper called the meeting to order, and introduced Moses Taylor, Esq., who said that, in behalf of the citizens of New York, he cordially welcomed Admiral Farragut to the metropolis. He believed that the sub-committee, who had first met the Admiral on board the Hartford, had already explained the programme which it had been determined to pursue, which left him little further to say.

Mr. Draper said: "At the request of the Chairman of the Merchants' Committee, I have the pleasure, Admiral Farragut, of reading to you the proceedings of the meeting held at this place yesterday evening:

Recognizing the illustrious service, heroic bravery, and tried loyalty which have distinguished the life of Rear-Admiral D. G. Farragut in the cause of his country—especially the lofty spirit of devotion by which he has been animated during all the period of the present war, and the signal victories achieved by him over the utmost skill and effort of the Rebellion; therefore

Resolved, That a committee of fifty citizens, to be named by the chair, with power to add to their number, be appointed to receive Admiral Farragut on his arrival, now soon expected, at this port.

Resolved, That a Federal salute be fired in honor of the arrival of the flag-ship Hartford with Admiral Farragut on board.

Resolved, That the city of New York, following the example of the great free cities of the world, in doing honor to their illustrious countrymen, honors itself by tendering to Admiral Farragut an invitation to become a resident thereof, and that the committee be appointed to devise the best mode of carrying this resolution into effect, so that the man, his achievements, and his fame may belong to the city.

Resolved, That we see with the highest satisfaction that the President, in his annual message, and the Secretary of the Treasury, recommend the creation of a higher grade of naval rank, with the designation of Admiral Farragut as the recipient, as a national recognition of distinguished service and exalted patriotism.

Resolved, That the offer made by the Collector, of a revenue cutter for the use of the committee in meeting the flag-ship Hartford, be accepted with thanks.

The reading of these resolutions was received with hearty applause at their conclusion.

Collector Draper then said:

"ADMIRAL FARRAGUT AND MEMBERS OF THE COMMITTEE: Thus far we have fulfilled the duty which has been assigned to us. The sub-committee have met the Hartford, and found on board her honored commander, Admiral Farragut, and his captain. We have performed that duty, on behalf of the committee, with feelings of pride and satisfaction; and, as representing a generous community, have endeavored to exhibit the gratitude of the entire nation, as expressed through this city, for the services and gallantry of the noble Admiral who is now before us. I shall say nothing more, Admiral Farragut, than to repeat what I have said to you this morning, that all our citizens, of every age and condition, receive you with open arms and heartfelt gratitude."

The Admiral arose and responded as follows:

"MY FRIENDS: I can only reply to you as I did before, by saying that I receive these compliments with great thankfulness and deep emotions. I am entirely unaccustomed to make such an address as I would desire to do upon this occasion; but, if I do not express what I think of the honor you do me, trust me I feel it most deeply. I don't think, however, that I particularly deserve any thing from your hands. I can merely say that I have done my duty to the best of my abilities. I have been devoted to the service of my country since I was eight years of age, and my father was devoted to it before me. I have not specially deserved these demonstrations of your regard. I owe every thing, perhaps, to chance, and to the praiseworthy exertions of my brother officers serving with me. That I have been fortunate is most true, and I am thankful, deeply thankful for it, for my country's sake. I return my thanks to the committee for their resolutions, especially for the one in regard to the creation of an additional rank."

The modest address of the Admiral was received with immense enthusiasm.

Captain Drayton, who will be remembered as a loyal South Carolinian, and as having distinguished himself in Dupont's victory at Hilton Head, where the rebel General Drayton (brother to the Captain), and commanding the forts, was ignominiously put to flight, arose upon his name being mentioned, and said:

"MY FRIENDS: I wish to remark how very grateful I feel to hear my name associated with that of Admiral Farragut. I merely happened to be in the Hartford when the Admiral won his glorious battles, and am deserving of no gratitude from you. Let me thank you for associating my name with the Admiral's."

Colonel A. J. H. Duganne then read the following

masterly and stirring ballad, which was listened to with breathless interest throughout, although the modest Admiral wore the appearance of being somewhat overwhelmed with eulogy:

FARRAGUT.

I.

Shipmates, together met
Now the first watch is set,
    Drain we a can to night:
God keep good sailors all!
Rest to the brave who fall!
God bless our Admiral,
    Leading the van to-night.
Soon, from yon Rebel spars,
Wearing the traitor's Bars,
We shall fling out the Stars,
    Blazoned with Stripes again!
High over battle scars,
    Liberty's types again!
Now may the song I bring,
Loud like a bugle ring:
FARRAGUT'S name I sing,—
    Fill up your pipes again!

II.

Down drops the setting sun;
Swift rolls the darkness on;
    Shipmates! the Night cometh!
Silent are trump and drum:
Silent are shot and bomb;

All the dark fleet is dumb—
    Dumb, till the fight cometh!
Messmates! we'll fill the can:
Life's but a little span;
Yonder's our battle-van—
    Yonder is Farragut:
Drink to the Iron Man—
    Drink to bold Farragut!
Shells be the cups we plight—
Cannons our beakers bright!
Blood be our wine to-night:
    Fill up to Farragut!

III.

Tell us, ye planets true!
Tell us, ye waters blue!
    Whither do eagles fly?
Out of what ocean's foam,
Out of what breaker's comb,
Born from what coral home,
    Soar up the sea-gulls high?
Then shall our answer rise
Higher than eagle flies,
Higher than sea-gull vies,
    Upward, with Farragut:
Upward, through Glory's skies,
    Sailing with Farragut!
He from the seas arose,
Grand with their deep repose;
White with their silver snows:
    God bless old Farragut!

IV.

Out of War's baptism,
Sprinkled with fire-chrism,
    Glory reveals her own;
Thus, like his namesake bold,
DAVID, renowned of old,
Boyhood, the Man foretold;
    Glory but sealed her own!
Scarce had twelve Summer suns
Passed him, like halcyons,
When with immortal ones
    Mingled young Farragut;
Breasting the British guns,
    Battled young Farragut!
Read ye our Hero-Scroll,
Shrined in the Capitol:
Fifty years back, its roll
    Bears the name—FARRAGUT!

V.

Shipmates! ye saw the man,
Leading our battle van,
    Calm and unfaltering:
Under Fort Jackson's hail;
Storming St. Philip's mail;
Fronting the Rebel gale,
    Stern and unaltering.
Groping through shadows gray,
Fought we our daring way;
Up through that gauntlet fray,
    Led by bold Farragut:

Castles and ships, at bay,
    Pounding on Farragut!
Oh! what a deed was done,
When the next morning's sun
Told us Orleans was won—
    Won by our Farragut!

VI.

Shipmates! ye've seen the waves
Building, from tropic caves,
    Columns gigantic;
Heard the great waters roar,
Where, on the angry shore,
Storm-ridden Labrador
    Braves the Atlantic:
But the seas never woke,
Never the thunder spoke,
Wild as the storm that broke
    Over bold Farragut—
Fierce as the battle-stroke
    Hurled against Farragut:
When, from those Rebel moats,
Up from those Rebel floats,
Six score of cannon throats
    Roared against Farragut!

VII.

Oh! how our hearts were chilled,
When the low words—"He's killed,"
    Some one had muttered;
Every pale mouth was shut,

Yet, with one meaning mute,
Asking for Farragut,
    Every lip fluttered.
Quickly, to calm the doubt,
"Farragut's here," we shout:
Then, what a cheer rang out—
    "Farragut! Farragut!"
High o'er the Rebel rout,
    "Three cheers for Farragut!"
Clear as our battle-cry,
Pealing up, wild and high,
Rending the murky sky—
    "Thank God for Farragut!"

VIII.

Mates! ye have heard full oft,
How, when he climbs aloft,
    Under the risen stars—
Soon, through the misty top,
Making our pulses stop,
Strange voices seem to drop
    Down from the mizzen-spars;
There, with bold PORTER, rides
HULL, of the "IRONSIDES;"
There, brave DECATUR glides
    Close to our Farragut—
High o'er all battle-tides
    Talking with Farragut!
Though the wild typhon pipes,
Though the fierce norther gripes,
Under the Stars and Stripes,
    There sits old Farragut!

IX.

So, when, from blazing ports,
Hurtling at Rebel forts
    Cannon-blows thunderous,
Down on MOBILE he led
War-ships, like dragons red,
While all the deep sea fled,
    Quaking, from under us:
Where the blue rockets flashed,
Where the hot shell was dashed,
Where the shot madly crashed,
    There we saw Farragut!
High at the mast-head lashed,
    There was old Farragut.
Castles once more we passed;
Ships on the shore we cast;
Lashed to our banner mast
    Still was bold Farragut!

X.

Messmates! at morn we fight:
This may be our last night;
    Fill up the can again!
If we must bravely fall,
God keep our dear ones all!
God shield the Admiral,
    Leading our van again!
When, o'er yon channel bars,
Stream out the rocket stars,
Then, to the signal spars,
    Up will climb Farragut:

Listening to cannon-jars,
There will be Farragut!
Wrapped in his battle-cloak,
Woven from fire and smoke,
God bless his heart of oak;
There we'll see FARRAGUT!

The poem was heartily applauded at the conclusion of its reading. Admiral Farragut then took the floor, and shook hands with the people as fast as they were introduced to him. He proceeded from the Custom House to the residence of a friend on Twenty-third Street, where Mrs. Farragut was expecting him.

You will recollect that when the last war with England opened, it found our navy in a sadly weak condition. It was so when the rebellion burst upon the country, but probably will never be again. We have always been afraid of large military organizations, acting almost as if we should have nothing more to do but shout "Independence now, and independence forever!" A careful observer at Washington, when Congress reassembled in the winter of 1864, wrote: "The prejudice against a standing army and a large navy has always been so great in this country that we have never completed the organization of either. In the army the only grades of generals we permitted were brigadier and major-generals. When we wanted to make Washington a full general, the proposition was opposed, and finally it took a special enactment to make him a lieutenant-general. Another law was required to raise Scott to the same rank, and still another for Grant; while the highest grade, that of full general, which all other large armies have, and which the rebels have had from the outset, we have not yet reached. So in the navy. Before the rebellion we didn't even have a commodore; and when Foote was sent to Cairo, and Dupont to Charleston, each in command of a squadron, we had no way of distinguishing them from any other of the captains in their fleets, excepting by calling them 'flag-officers.' Finally the last Congress, in a bill reorganizing the navy, made what it thought a wonderful step forward, and authorized commodores and rear-admirals. There still remain two higher ranks, common to the navies of all civilized countries—'vice-admiral' and full 'admiral'; while in some navies, as in the British, there are three grades again of full admirals, distinguished by the colors of their pennants. In his forthcoming message, the President will recommend an advance of one grade in the navy, similar to that given the army last session, in the revival of the lieutenant-generalship. The new grade will be that of vice-admiral; and immediately on its creation, the Navy Department will recommend, and the President will nominate to the vice-admiralty, the Salamander of the navy, Rear-Admiral Farragut."

On December 22, 1864, a bill creating the naval grade was introduced into the Senate and passed, when it went to the House of Representatives, and was also unanimously accepted there. The following day it was signed by the President, who at once nominated Rear-Admiral Farragut to the position, which appointment was immediately confirmed by the Senate, without the usual formality of referring it to a standing committee. Vice-Admiral Farragut, who was in New York, was immediately notified by telegraph of the mark of distinction conferred upon him.

The rank of vice-admiral, which has been conferred upon Farragut, bears some resemblance to the rank of lieutenant-general, which was conferred upon Grant. The position, however, differs, we suppose, in this: that while Grant, as lieutenant-general, has command of all the armies of the United States, wherever they may be operating, Farragut, as rear-admiral, will not have command of all the naval forces of the United States. It is practicable for one officer, in a central position, to command or direct all the land forces; but it would hardly be practicable for one officer to command all the naval forces on the Atlantic, the Gulf, and the inland rivers He might, it is true, under the Secretary of the Navy, give a general direction to naval operations, but we do not understand that his duties in the future are to be of this character. He will still continue to serve his country and glorify his flag from the deck of the "dear old Hartford."

"The deep and admiring feeling of the people was, that Congress and President have seldom done any thing so entirely pleasing to 'all hands of us'—as one of the Hartford's tars would say—as the establishment of the rate or grade of vice-admiral, and the promotion of the brave Farragut to that new rank.

"In Farragut the ideal sailor, the seaman of Nelson's and Collingwood's days, is revived; and the feeling of the people toward him is of the same peculiar character as that which those great and simple-hearted naval heroes of Great Britain evoked in the hearts of their countrymen. In these days of steam-engines and iron-armor, the good old race of seamen threatens to die out—to be superseded by mechanics and engineers. For the Monitors a blacksmith is more important, in the general opinion, than the best sailor that ever reefed top-sails or hove the lead; and an engineer need not be very conceited to fancy himself as important to a modern frigate as her first lieutenant. But Farragut has shown to the naval world that the virtues of the old school, the qualities which distinguished Blake, Nelson, Decatur, Preble, and Hull, long before steam-engines and iron-sides were thought of, are as necessary and effectual to-day as ever.

"Nor is the country ill-pleased that the old spirit, which made our little navy famous in the war of 1812, asserts itself, and approves itself, in these later days, and among these later contrivances; and surely to the seamen of the old school it is a glorious pledge that their profession will live, and its peculiar virtues remain valuable, no matter by what accidents the conditions of the combat are changed. Dauntless bravery and the fertility in expedients which is born of the never-ceasing and ever-changing conditions of life on the ocean, compel victory now as ever. Farragut has shown the falsity of the belief entertained by some here, and by many abroad, that hereafter a sea-fight is to be only a work of 'main strength and stupidness'—to use a sailor's phrase."

The modesty with which the Admiral bore his honors was characteristic of the man, to whom *duty* was a word more awakening to his unselfish ambition, than *fame.*

CHAPTER XIX.

A Festival—The Merchants of New York and the Vice-Admiral—The Testimonial—Correspondence—Farragut at Richmond—At Norfolk—A Noble Speech—Visits other Places—Vice-Admiral Farragut compared with Naval Heroes of the past—His True Greatness—A Poet's Offering.

DECEMBER 21st, the New England Society in New York celebrated the landing of the Pilgrim Fathers at Plymouth two hundred and forty-four years before, at the Astor House. The dining-hall was richly decorated for the occasion, and presented a brilliant spectacle. As our Admiral was among the guests, a sketch of the exciting scenes will have an unusual attraction.

Upon the tables were ornamented pieces representing the landing on Plymouth Rock, the ship Mayflower, Miles Standish, a New England cottage, a Temple of Liberty, etc. The President of the Society, Mr. Henry A. Hurlbut, presided at the festive board. "New England, I Love Thee," was sung by a glee club, at the close of which Vice-Admiral Farragut entered the dining-room, and was hailed with nine cheers from the audience, who simultaneously arose and greeted him with the wildest enthusiasm. Captain Drayton, who accompanied Admiral Farragut, was also greeted with cheers, and both gentlemen were furnished with seats at the head of the table, on the right of the President.

After the excitement had subsided Mr. William C. Bryant was called upon to respond to the fifth regular toast, and said: "He wished, for his part, that all the poets of New England were present, to listen to the praise that had been bestowed on him. It was a theory with some historians that the history of nations had its origin in poetry." He compared the rude strains of the poets of the pilgrimage with the poetry of New England of the present day. We were now drifting into the purity of refined poetry. The poets of New England are worthy of the high praise that is accorded to the inspiration that fills their verse. He rejoiced that he lived in an age when heroism was coincident with humanity. He thanked God in his providence he had not destined the country to short duration, but that He had destined it for a long duration of peace and victory.

After the reading of a letter from General Grant, the President called upon Vice-Admiral Farragut, who, on rising, was greeted with the most boisterous applause. He said: "Gentlemen, I do not know what your expectations may be of Vice-Admiral Farragut, but I have seen enough of Rear-Admiral Farragut to know that he is not very well qualified to make such a speech as you would wish to listen to. I am happy to return my thanks for the hospitable reception and enthusiastic honor I have always received in this hall. When I saw you last, I promised to go abroad as soon as possible, to keep up a sympathetic feeling with your association in another quarter. I only wish I could return my thanks as the General has done by a letter; but we have some odd notions in the navy; and one is, that we share our shot as we do our prize-money, and the higher the rank the greater is the responsibility; and hence I suppose I am called upon. I can back up what the gentleman (Mr. Bryant) has said of the manner in which the sons of New England, as well as of other States, have poured out their blood in the South. God knows they have poured it out freely."

As Admiral Farragut took his seat there were loud calls for Captain Winslow, who responded by saying that he could only repeat the thanks expressed by Vice-Admiral Farragut at the warm reception that had been extended to him.

Captain Drayton was then loudly called for. In response, he said that there was an old idea in the navy, that no navy officer could speak. He thought that the reverse had been shown to-night. His great fortune lay in his association with Admiral Farragut, for anybody who came in contact with him caught a little of his spirit.

www.ingramcontent.com/pod-product-compliance
Lightning Source LLC
LaVergne TN
LVHW020233110826
845151LV00003B/913

* 9 7 8 1 4 2 5 5 3 6 9 3 0 *